SEEKING JUSTICE

Ethics and
International Affairs

Titles in This Series

Case Studies in International Affairs
Series Editor: Martin Staniland, University of Pittsburgh

The case-study approach to teaching and learning is on the rise in foreign policy and international studies classrooms. Westview Press is pleased to promote this trend by publishing a series of casebooks for a variety of college courses.

Innovative educators are using case studies to:

- Develop critical thinking skills
- Engage students in decisionmaking and role playing
- Transform lecture courses into interactive courses
- Encourage students to apply theoretical concepts using practical experience and knowledge
- Exercise skills in negotiation, management, and leadership

Each book will include theoretical and historical background material, four to eight case studies from all regions of the world, material introducing and connecting the cases, and discussion questions. Teaching notes will be provided to adopting professors, and to encourage the use of several different books and themes within a single class, the casebooks will be short, inexpensive paperbacks of approximately 150 pages.

The individual case studies making up the heart of each volume were developed in conjunction with seven institutions—University of Pittsburgh, Harvard University, Georgetown University, Columbia University, Johns Hopkins University, University of Southern California, and the International Peace Academy—under the auspices of The Pew Charitable Trusts. From over 140 case studies developed by leading scholars, the editors have selected those studies that thematically and substantively offer the best classroom examples for each topic in the series.

SEEKING JUSTICE

Ethics and
International Affairs

edited by
RACHEL M. McCLEARY

United States Institute of Peace

Westview Press

BOULDER ■ SAN FRANCISCO ■ OXFORD

Case Studies in International Affairs

This volume, as compiled, copyright © 1992 by Westview Press, Inc. The following case studies have been edited and are reprinted here with permission: "'Just Cause'? The 1989 United States Invasion of Panama" by Christopher Tatham and Rachel McCleary (Pew case study no. 461) copyright © by The Pew Charitable Trusts; "The Vietnam Negotiations, October–December 1972" by Allan E. Goodman (Pew case study no. 307) copyright © by The Pew Charitable Trusts; "The United States and the Law of the Sea Treaty" by Steven R. David and Peter Digeser (Pew case study no. 418) copyright © by The Pew Charitable Trusts; "Reaching Agreement with the IMF: The Nigerian Negotiations, 1983–1986" by Thomas J. Biersteker (Pew case study no. 205) copyright © by The Pew Charitable Trusts; "European Community Enlargement and the United States" by John Odell and Margit Matzinger-Tchakerian (Pew case study no. 130) copyright © by The Pew Charitable Trusts; "Development Strategies in Conflict: Brazil and the Future of the Amazon" by Rachel McCleary (Carnegie Council on Ethics and International Affairs case study no. 1) (Pew case study no. 501) copyright © by Carnegie Council on Ethics and International Affairs.

Published in 1992 in the United States of America by Westview Press, Inc., 5500 Central Avenue, Boulder, Colorado 80301-2877, and in the United Kingdom by Westview Press, 36 Lonsdale Road, Summertown, Oxford OX2 7EW

Library of Congress Cataloging-in-Publication Data
Seeking Justice : Ethics and international affairs /
    edited by Rachel M. McCleary.
      p. cm. — (Case studies in international affairs)
    Includes bibliographical references.
    ISBN 0-8133-8058-8 (hc) — ISBN 0-8133-8059-6 (pb)
    1. International relations—Moral and ethical aspects.
I. McCleary, Rachel M., 1953–   . II. Series.
JX1395.E82   1992
172′4—dc20   90-44887
                                                                        CIP

Printed and bound in the United States of America

The paper used in this publication meets the requirements of the American National Standard for Permanence of Paper for Printed Library Materials Z39.48-1984.

10   9   8   7   6   5   4   3   2   1

CONTENTS

FOREWORD

The Westview series Case Studies in International Affairs stems from a major project of The Pew Charitable Trusts entitled "The Pew Diplomatic Initiative." Launched in 1985, this project has sought to improve the teaching and practice of negotiation through adoption of the case method of teaching, principally in professional schools of international affairs in the United States.

By 1989, authors associated with the seven institutions involved in the Diplomatic Initiative had written over 140 case studies in international negotiation for classroom use.[1] In considering a second phase of the program, The Pew Charitable Trusts determined that its emphasis should shift from writing cases to encouraging their adoption in courses taught through the case method.

One aspect of this phase has been the establishment of a clearinghouse at the Graduate School of Public and International Affairs, University of Pittsburgh, to distribute and promote the cases. During the first two years of the clearinghouse's operation, it quickly became clear that a sizeable market for the case studies (and a considerable interest in case-method teaching) existed in the larger community of university and college undergraduate instruction. By October 1990, over 15,000 single copies of cases had been sold, and the circle of customers had widened to include instructors in such countries as India, Bulgaria, and the former Soviet Union.

It also became clear that, although a classroom use for individual cases would always exist, there was instructional potential in sets of cases selected to illustrate particular issues in negotiation as well as negotiations over particular policy matters. Hence the Westview series, which offers students and instructors the opportunity to examine and discuss specific themes, including themes (such as foreign policymaking) that fall outside of the ambit of international negotiation. Each volume presents a selection of cases, some short, others long, some essentially unchanged, others extensively edited or rewritten. Each volume also contains an introductory chapter, identifying the characteristic features and dilemmas of the kind of negotiation or issue exemplified by the cases. Each volume contains questions for discussion and suggestions for simulation and further reading.

Case-method teaching typically involves two elements. The first (and essential) element is careful reading of a case document by students. The second is one or more classroom sessions in which an instructor, using sustained Socratic questioning, tries to get students to explore the meaning of events that are described, but deliberately not interpreted or explained, in the case document.

Like all teaching, case-method teaching depends on a contract, however implicit. The contract here is framed by two norms: the first is that the material within the case provides a common stock of evidence and an obligatory point of reference. If this norm is broken by the introduction of extraneous or privileged information, the case will cease to serve as a common focus, the assumption of equal information (however artificial and fictitious it may be) will break down, and some students will feel discouraged from participating.

The second norm is one of judgmental equality—that, for purposes of the discussion, the instructor willingly suspends his or her authority for the sake of encouraging students to develop and express their own interpretations of events. Although the instructor may (indeed, should) organize discussions so as to lead students into specific questions, he or she will undermine the exploratory and interactive character of the discussions if students have the impression that they are required to discover "the right answers." This does not mean that instructors have to say (much less to believe) that they have no opinions or that one person's opinion is as good as another's. It simply means that they should be prepared to retreat, temporarily, to the roles of agenda-setter and discussion leader, rather than assuming those of decisionmaker and interpreter.

Although obviously there are some important premises regarding educational philosophy and psychology underpinning belief in case-method teaching, the case for instructors holding back is essentially pragmatic—that discussion is a good educational vehicle and that students will only climb onto it if they are allowed to share in the driving.

Case-method teaching is, then, a tool, supplementing the conventional tools of exposition. Cases can be used to follow up lectures; they can (as this series implies) be used comparatively; they can be used for discussion or for simulation. They can be used with or without accompanying writing assignments. They can be used to illustrate theoretical concepts (such as power) or to require students to enter into the agonies of political choice ("What would you have done if you were President Carter?"). But what they invariably do is to enable—and to force—students to take responsibility for their own political and academic education. The faint burning smell of hard thinking hangs in the air after a good case discussion has taken place. Surely anything that produces that smell should be welcome.

Martin Staniland
Series Editor

NOTES

1. The institutions concerned were the School of International Relations, University of Southern California; the School of International and Public Affairs, Columbia University; the Edmund A. Walsh School of Foreign Service, Georgetown University; the John F. Kennedy School of Government, Harvard University; the International Peace Academy (of the United Nations); the Paul H. Nitze School of Advanced International Studies, Johns Hopkins University; and the Graduate School of Public and International Affairs, University of Pittsburgh.

1

INTRODUCTION

From advocating the preservation of the Amazonian rain forest to supporting the military deposition of the dictator of another country, citizens and their governments engage in policies that extend beyond political boundaries. Questions about the justness and political legitimacy of these policies are raised but are frequently waylaid in favor of expediency and practicality. Yet national security issues regarding traditional military concerns, such as protection of one's borders, and, more recently, concerning the degradation of the environment, for example, pollution of the atmosphere, are increasingly bringing countries into conflict.[1] As each country seeks to assert its political sovereignty, maintain territorial integrity, and protect domestic interests, pressures among states mount, creating the need for responsive, flexible, and effective means of forging international consensus.

This volume deals with issues at the interface of the nature of state sovereignty, the legitimacy of domestic political arrangements, and the behavior of international orders and institutions in international affairs.[2] The focus is on the ethical aspects of the means and ends chosen and pursued by various actors in international affairs and on the issues of distributive justice that arise from their interactions in the international arena.

The ordering of the cases in this volume is intentional. Presented initially is the case involving the invasion of Panama by the United States. Following this is a study that considers the Vietnamese peace negotiations. Each case raises questions about the *morality of means*. Both cases grapple with the important ethical dilemmas arising with the use of violence and deception in international affairs. In their examinations of the ethical reasons for limiting the use of violence and deception, readers are invited to decide, given the circumstances, if their use was morally justified.

1

Integral to determining the limits of morally questionable means is the topic of political legitimacy, both on the domestic and international level. Domestically, political legitimacy is the notion that commonly recognized laws, norms, and practices exist by which the actions of public officials are judged by the people to be acceptable or not acceptable. When the United States used military power to depose Panama's General Manuel Antonio Noriega, publicly elected officials acted on behalf of the American people. Do citizens implicitly consent to the use of coercive means by their government when they elect politicians to office?

The political legitimacy of the invasion of Panama and the arrest of General Noriega by U.S. troops is determined, first, at the domestic level by the degree of accountability between the government and its people. Citizens of a country consent to certain types of military aggression on the part of their government, for example, in defense of their country against foreign intervention. The use of military force as a form of coercion in the domestic affairs of another state is different, however, because it raises questions about the government's use of morally questionable means and about the limits citizens believe ought to be placed on the use of those means.

Military intervention in the domestic affairs of another state also raises questions about the inviolability of states. Once citizens approve of their government's military intervention, they expose their own society to the possibility of foreign intervention. This leads us to the second level of political legitimacy, in the international arena.

Political legitimacy at the international level is determined according to the dictates of agreements and interpretations of the rules and regulations governing international institutions. For example, the charters of the United Nations (UN) and the Organization of American States (OAS) explicitly provide for respect for the sovereignty of states and for nonintervention in the domestic affairs of member states.[3] Member states frequently violate these recognized rules in pursuit of self-interested goals. In response to aberrant behavior on the part of a member state, the international organization can impose on it economic sanctions and other forms of coercive punishment. As a case in point, the United Nations Security Council imposed trade and economic sanctions on Iraq for its military invasion of Kuwait in 1990. The Security Council stipulated that part of the revenues from Iraq's oil sales were to be compensation for Kuwaiti victims of the invasion.

Other types of international agreements by which political legitimacy can be measured are international regimes, such as the Montreal Protocol. Regimes are specialized agreements that commit signatories to comply with specific requirements, such as reducing the emission of environmentally damaging chemicals within their borders. Compared to international regimes, international orders are broad and informal networks of activity. For example, international economic and trade markets are frameworks in which states, multilateral institutions, corporations, banks, and other actors are free to participate as buyers and sellers. Specialized agreements, such as the General Agreement on Tariffs and Trade (GATT), regulate specific trade and economic activities within those frameworks. Like international organizations, international regimes explicitly provide for sanctions in the event that a member state violates acknowledged rules and regulations.

Presented next are a case study involving the Law of the Sea Treaty, followed by a case study that concerns the International Monetary Fund (IMF) and Nigeria. Both of these cases raise questions about the *morality of ends*. International regimes, such as the UN Law of the Sea Treaty, and international organizations, such as the IMF, were established with certain agreed-upon rules in mind. These rules advance certain ends that cannot be separated from the functioning of the international regime or organization. These two cases invite the reader to question how institutional rules contributed to the outcome of the negotiating process and whether or not that outcome was just.

Some public officials consider an outcome to be just if it maximizes the general welfare. Others do not accept this utilitarian view of justice but rather argue that a more egalitarian distribution of benefits is a just outcome. What constitutes a fair outcome? This question needs to be considered within the context of the empirical and political conditions constraining the negotiating process.

Next, we proffer the European Community Enlargement case study; and, finally, a case study about Brazil. These two cases show the limits of international treaties and institutions in dealing with questions of *distributive justice*. Traditionally, morality in international relations has been viewed by public officials as a constraining force in their pursuit of national interest. Morality, many argue, impedes their ability to act in the best interests of the state. Is national security so paramount that public officials can ignore the ethical considerations and conventions of international organizations whenever it is expedient to protect their national interests? The last two cases suggest the opposite: *Morality*, in the form of distributive justice, provides reasonable grounds for looking beyond national interest in order to act to meet the interests of participating nations; recognizing that to act single-mindedly in the pursuit of one's national interest will result in policies that not only do not meet anyone's goals but also could very well be detrimental to one's future interests.

THE REQUIREMENTS OF DISTRIBUTIVE JUSTICE

When national interest is not adequate for determining distributive patterns (for example, who has fishing rights in certain seas) then what standard should be used? In international affairs, promoting the national interest is the overriding and legitimate goal of a nation's leaders. Yet the moral skeptic's worldview, that states are independent actors pursuing their own national interests unconstrained by legal and moral principles, is not reflective of how states function in the contemporary international system nor of the international pressures often placed on governments when making domestic policy.

Issues raised in the various cases presented in this book invite the reader to examine existing distribution patterns of goods and the outcomes of those patterns in light of distributive justice. What constitutes an equitable allocation of the burdens and benefits of distributive practices? Should the rich nations of the world be required to share their affluence with the poor nations? What obligations, if any, do industrialized nations have to transfer environmentally safe technology to developing countries? Should the major polluters of global resources pay for the cleanup and preservation of natural resources?

Justice is the measure by which the distribution of goods can be equitably decided. Is the distribution just when it is done according to equality? ability? social utility? productivity? or when it applies to basic needs such as food, shelter, or clothing? supply and demand? The distribution of goods, such as fishing rights in the open seas, is just according to an equitable allocation of the rights among nations. In this sense, distributive justice is concerned with the ethical nature of means: In what way and to what extent can nations fairly divide the resources of the open seas for each nation's benefit and profit?

Notice that insofar as we are concerned with means, distributive justice is a method of allocating fishing rights in a fair manner. But nations, under a just distribution, could exploit fishing rights until the fish are extinct. Consider the case of certain fishing fleets using drift nets that indiscriminately catch many species, thereby depleting the numbers of fish in the oceans and endangering ocean life. The allocation of fishing rights needs to be reconsidered given this alarming exploitation of marine life.

One way of reassessing the distribution of fishing rights is to examine the history of the distribution practices. How did the distribution practice come into existence?[4] In this sense, justice is backward-looking. It is embedded in historical practices and institutions that were initiated at a different time and in a different social context, by historical accident or design. The moral legitimacy of the practices and institutions, however, needs to be scrutinized in light of contemporary events and empirical conditions.

All nations share in the exploitation of the open seas. Yet the mutual end they seek is not the extinction of marine life but the continuing exploitation of it as a source of food. The end that drives the international distribution of fishing rights is the value ocean life has to each nation as a renewable resource. Distributive justice, then, is also concerned with the ethical nature of ends that drive the patterns of distribution: What ends do we seek to pursue when we set up institutions and create patterns of distribution?

In this sense, justice is forward-looking. It is abstract and ahistorical, lifting the individual or institution out of the social context in an attempt to identify and define universally moral ends. What goods should we distribute more equitably in order to have international regimes and institutions that allow sovereign states to function to protect the interests of their citizens yet also share resources with others? If all nations agreed that they value ocean life as a renewable resource, then they would have a foundation for agreeing that a just distribution of fishing rights requires outlawing the use of drift nets.

Certainly we believe that people have a right to food, shelter, clothing, and healthcare, and we believe these types of goods ought to be distributed equitably among peoples of the world. There are other kinds of goods, however, such as freedom, equality, and the enhancement of human capabilities, that also need to be equitably distributed through the practices of institutions and international orders. The World Bank, through its funding of development projects, seeks to promote what it calls "human development." Human development is the "enlarging of people's choice . . . to lead a long and healthy life, to acquire knowledge and to have access to resources needed for a decent standard of living."[5] The just or unjustness of the institutional practices promoted by the World Bank can be assessed in terms of how the institution's staff goes about fulfilling these human goods.

The ends that are valued by institutions and societies drive the distributive patterns that are employed by the people and institutions. These ends can only be identified by examining the nature and very existence of the institutions, regimes, and societies that engage and perpetuate them. The just or unjustness of institutional practices can also be determined in light of the ultimate human goods we value.

In an analysis of the ethical nature of means and ends and the justness of distributive patterns in global affairs, the means that are justified, the ends that are pursued, and the distributive patterns that are chosen are assessed within the framework of an ethical approach. It is from a particular ethical standpoint that actions and policies may be justified. How one analyzes the relevance of empirical conditions and what formal conditions ought to inform the decision depends upon the ethical perspective one takes.

FOUR ETHICAL APPROACHES

Various approaches to international political theory attempt to sort out the ethical limitations of state sovereignty in international affairs and the demands justice places on peoples and their governments to assist others. Four principal approaches are presented in this chapter: moral skepticism, the morality of states, communitarianism, and the cosmopolitan view. Each conception is useful in framing questions about the ethical nature and the implications of decisions, actions, and policies presented in the case studies. Each ethical approach emphasizes different aspects of issues. The varying conceptions offer different ethical parameters to determine whether or not policies and their implementations are seen as morally permissible; and whether they are viewed as just or unjust. The case studies are presented in such a way as to allow the reader to apply the various approaches to the issues at hand.

MORAL SKEPTICISM

Moral skepticism, as developed by Thomas Hobbes, is the position that morality and normative considerations have no application or significance in international relations.[6] Acting according to moral standards is against the interests of a state because there exist no assurances, in the form of an impartial, international authority, that nations will take into account the interests of other states and respect and protect those interests. But more fundamentally, according to the moral skeptic, there exists no international consensus on a standard of justice. Even if there were such a consensus, or even if nations were willing to abide by the status quo, the lack of an international authority, or what Thomas Hobbes called a "common power," to ensure that nations abide by the same standard of justice means that any nation voluntarily soliciting cooperation from other nations compromises its own interests.

Another danger exists, according to the skeptic, in promoting international cooperation and consensus. In an attempt to make aberrant nations abide by an international standard of justice, an international authority such as the United Nations peacekeeping mechanism would have to be appointed. The function of this authority would be to mediate and resolve disputes between nations. However, it could well lose sight of its role as peacekeeper and enforcer of international standards. It could become an international police power intervening in the sovereign affairs of states—for example, in cases of civil war or government-sponsored genocide—or it could easily try to impose its standards of right and wrong on the domestic affairs of nations. Nations could not trust the international authority to solely mediate and enforce an international consensus on relations among states. Thus, the skeptic warns, a nation that determines its foreign policy by considering the interests of other nations is, in the final analysis, willing "to expose [it]self to prey."[7]

Nevertheless, there will be times when leaders of a state perceive it to be in the interests of their nation's security and prosperity to have international cooperation. There may also be occasions when they feel that it would be good for public morale to have the state engage in humanitarian assistance. But, the skeptic cautions, however many times a state may want to pursue longer term goals, the state will refrain from doing so, not because there is an absence of self-interest but out of fear that the industrialized or militarily superior nations will do as they please. This is known as the free-rider problem.

The free-rider problem arises when at least one state (or a group of states) stands to gain benefits by not cooperating with the others, although the other states are continuing to cooperate with each other.[8] For example, the majority of nations of the world voluntarily agreed in 1990 to amend the Convention on International Trade of Endangered Species (CITES) to include a ban on all ivory trade. The purpose of the ban is to save the African elephant from extinction. In 1970 African elephant herds contained approximately 2.5 million animals. Today it is estimated that 350,000 African elephants are left. China is not a signatory of CITES yet it is benefiting from noncompliance with the ban in two ways. First, China is continuing to trade in ivory, thereby maintaining its economic benefit. Second, China benefits from the repopulation of the herds at the expense of other nations that are abiding by the ban on ivory trade.[9]

The free-rider problem is exacerbated by the fact that states are unequal in terms of geographic size and shape, natural resources, polity, economic and trade systems, technology, material needs, and cultural homogeneity. Empirical conditions, or what Hobbes calls the state of nature, create an environment in which nations compete against each other on an unequal footing for resources and security. Developing countries, as a result, are often placed in the defensive posture of attempting to protect their interests by asserting their sovereignty and expanding sovereign claims over resources in order to fend off aggressive actions by more powerful states. The United States and other maritime powers, for instance, support an international regime based on freedom of the seas that allows for maximum national access to the high seas. Developing countries, in contrast, have sought to extend their sovereignty over ocean waters in order to insure national control over fisheries, minerals in the oceans, and to keep foreign military vessels away from their shores. These countries cannot compete with the large factory fishing ships of the industrialized countries. Further, they lack the technology for mining the seabed, the power to keep foreign military ships and submarines away from shore, and the technology to clean up marine pollution from oil tankers. Rather than seeking to form cooperative international regimes and institutions, developing states are relying on sovereignty and self-interest to compete with wealthier and technologically superior nations for their share of material resources. Empirical conditions in international relations dictate that self-interest guide national policy and place preservation of the state above international cooperation and consensus.

Why, then, should we concern ourselves with issues of justice in international affairs? Even though, for a moral skeptic, justice does not apply to relations among nations, there are times when a country may act not to promote its own interests directly but to engage in acts of charity so that its citizens can "feel good." Self-interest is the baseline for measuring the costs and benefits to the nation and for assessing the risks of engaging in foreign assistance.

As long as the provision of humanitarian aid incurs minimal costs to the nation, and the interests of the nation are not harmed, the skeptic can justify the enterprise. Humanitarian assistance, like a military invasion, can be a form of intervention in the internal affairs of another state. It becomes a form of intervention when it is deliberately chosen as a means of limiting the sovereignty and self-reliance of another state. For example, a state can deliberately choose to give food aid to a country afflicted by famine in order to make that state obligated to it.[10] Unless effort is put into indigenous food production, the famine-afflicted country will enter a cycle of food dependency that will persist for some time. From the skeptic's point of view, humanitarian assistance, such as food aid, is not a matter of acting on moral principle to help starving people. The primary policy objective of the leaders of a nation, then, is to further the preservation of the state by whatever means that prove to be beneficial, and that includes humanitarian assistance. All other objectives are subject to a cost-benefit analysis (in which the risks and costs to the nation can never exceed the benefits).

DISCUSSION QUESTIONS

1. *Is it irrational to abide by a standard of justice in the absence of a realistic expectation that other nations will do the same?*
2. *Is a "common power" needed to assure that each state will follow the same rules of conduct in international affairs?*
3. *Are some compromises and risks to national self-interest necessary in order to achieve longer term goals?*

THE MORALITY OF STATES

According to the morality of states position, the state remains the arena in which civil and political liberties are defined and protected.[11] To attempt to create an international standard of justice would be to deny the political process by which the rights of people come into being, are defined, and are protected. To create an international morality that is maintained above the state would be to destroy the source of justice itself, the community.

From this viewpoint, the state is not a political, legal representative of the community, it *is* the community. The union of the people and the government makes up the state. The state obtains its moral and political legitimacy from the rights that individual men and women possess "to live as members of a historic community and to express their inherited culture through political forms worked out among themselves."[12] From a perspective internal to the state, the legitimacy of a government as the representative of its people is qualitatively different from the legitimacy of a state vis-à-vis other states.

States, as members of an international society, are legitimate as long as they possess territorial integrity and political sovereignty (i.e., a stable political entity that controls its people). Other nations recognize a state as sovereign, be it a tyranny or a democracy, because it is a self-determining community—the government successfully exercises control over the affairs of the population. Thus, unlike the skeptic, the statist view holds that there are two rules (albeit broad ones) governing relations among states: respect for sovereignty and nonintervention in the domestic affairs of a sovereign state.

The domestic legitimacy of a state is determined by the "fit" between the government and the community, that is, "the degree to which the government actually represents the political life of the people."[13] A state is considered by other states to be legitimate as long as the fit exists between the government and the people it governs. The state, according to this view, constitutes the only viable form of political society in that it is the political entity that protects the peoples' right to self-determination, to live in a civil society of their own choosing and making. When the civil and political liberties of citizens are oppressed by the government, the fit between the government and its people becomes questionable and foreign intervention becomes possible.

Issues of justice in international affairs, (e.g., invading another country) are determined by the standard of justice that arises within a community. The moral and political legitimacy of a foreign policy of a state can be judged only by its citizens according to their own domestic standards of right and wrong. Principles that apply to international relations are derived from a standard of domestic morality by analogy. These principles are relevant to international affairs insofar as they are relevant to what is considered morally and politically legitimate by the community.

Within this view, intervention is considered to be justified when foreigners are able to determine that the government no longer fulfills its political functions: to defend its people against foreigners, to prevent constraints and repression of the people's common life, to foster civil liberties, and to permit political and economic freedom. Foreign intervention, however, is not solely justified on the moral ground that a government is harming its citizens—as in the case of government-sponsored genocide. From the statist point of view, foreign intervention in such a case is justified on political grounds when the state is no longer fulfilling certain obligations it has to its people, obligations that other states recognize as part of what it means to be a legitimate political entity in international affairs.

Intervention by a state in the internal affairs of another is permissible when

1. a political community within the state is in active revolt. In other words, a political community rebels against its government, claiming that it no longer represents community interests.
2. another state has already militarily intervened on behalf of the revolting faction. Other states may then legitimately intervene to counterbalance the first intervention.
3. the violations of human rights committed by the established government within the state are so extreme that it is absurd to speak of a fit existing between the government and its people. Human rights violations considered extreme enough to warrant foreign intervention are of three types: the massacre of citizens at the order of the government, the enslavement of people by their government, and the mass expulsion of people by their government.[14]

Thus, unlike the skeptic who considers foreign policy choices in light of national self-interest, the statist allows for some occasions when humanitarian intervention is politically legitimate and morally justified. In other words, there are conditions under which a foreigner is able to judge and criticize the political legitimacy of a domestic regime and to determine that humanitarian intervention is warranted.

However, deciding when the fit between government and its people is no longer legitimate is not easily determined. An individual country's circumstances rarely allow for a clear-cut analysis. Is a government actively repressing its citizens by the use of force, or is it defending itself against destabilization efforts by a foreign power? In addition, a government may be performing well in terms of spurring the nation's economic growth but at the same time it may be severely repressing the country's civil and political liberties.

Empirically, an individual country's circumstances vary and are open to interpretation by member states of the international society. Conceptually, the notion of what constitutes the fit between government and its people, namely the state, is also ambiguous. To what does the word "state" refer? First, there is the notion of "community," which refers to "a body of people organized into a political, municipal or social unity."[15] The notion of community encompasses a wide variety of social arrangements. It could be a moral or religious community that shares a commonly acknowledged value system, for example, the Hasidic Jews who are geographically dispersed and not linked by personal ties. A community could also be a legal community, such as a township or a professional association. Because the notion of community is so broad, identifying what the fit is in a community and when the fit no longer exists varies with the kind of social arrangement under consideration.

Second, a state could be a nation. A nation is "a stable, historically developed community of people with a territory, economic life, distinctive culture, and language in common."[16] Before the 1800s, the term "nation" referred to one's birth and descent group. Many nations could live within the borders of a political entity such as a province or state. Today, many nations of Amerindians live within the borders of states such as Brazil, Canada, and the United States.

In modern usage, the term "nation" has come to signify an aggregate of persons who enjoy political independence and unity.[17] The nation, in this political sense, became associated with the idea of governance and territorial integrity. The American colonists shared language and culture with the British, yet nation for the colonists meant a distinct government and territory.[18]

The lack of fit in a nation is difficult to identify because neither is a nation a geographically homogeneous group nor does it refer to equal political representation for all members of the group. If one ethnic nation is dominant among many, imposing its cultural and moral values on other nations, does the fit exist? When is a nation a legitimate political entity?

Third, there is the notion of a state. The state is defined as "the body politic as organized for supreme civil rule and government; the political organization which is the basis of civil government; hence the supreme civil power and government vested in a country or nation."[19] For the statist perspective, the state is the community, not merely a representation of it. When the civil rights of citizens are violated by a government, does the fit no longer exist? How does the government constitute the legitimate representative of the people? If a political form of representation, for example, a totalitarian government, is exercised, does the fit between government and people exist?

As a result of our inability to clearly determine the nature of domestic circumstances and arrangements of a state, trade and other forms of interaction between states are not contingent upon the just or unjust nature of the relationship between a government and its people. According to the statist position, there are equally numerous examples of corrupt democratic regimes violating human rights as there are cases of benevolent dictatorships economically performing well. Within this view, lending funds by the International Monetary Fund to a repressive totalitarian regime is no different from lending to a multiparty democratic society.

Issues of domestic governance—such as the exercise of control over a society by a political authority, the management of economic, social, and natural resources, and how the administration of these resources contributes to the poverty and landlessness of people—are irrelevant to decisions regarding relations between states. For the right to a decent standard of living, the right to own property, the right to equal opportunity, and the right to obtain an education are rights defined within and by a state; and these kinds of rights are only legitimate and enforceable within the context of that state.

DISCUSSION QUESTIONS

1. *Some states, such as Kenya, are made up of various communities or "nations" in the form of tribes. Can the statist definition of a state accommodate the domestic problems faced by many contemporary states with heterogeneous populations?*
2. *Within the statist view, does every nation have a right to peacefully secede from the state and form its own sovereign entity?*
3. *The statist speaks of a "fit" or union between the people and the government. How is domestic political legitimacy defined within this view?*
4. *On what moral and political grounds are we to decide when there no longer exists a fit between a government and its people? When are the violations of citizens' liberties and human rights so egregious that the fit between government and its people no longer exists?*

COMMUNITARIANISM

The limits of justice, within a communitarian view, are determined neither by the geographic boundaries of a state nor by the fit between the government and its people. Rather, the extent of the domain of justice and its content are determined by the social, economic, and political relationships of a community.[20] How resources are to be allocated and conflicts resolved are determined by the members of the community from the perspective of the social relationships and the obligations and responsibilities that arise therein.

The community, for the communitarian, is defined in terms of membership and relationship. The Yanomami tribe of Amazonia, the residents of a city, the representatives to the United Nations, the citizens of China, all are members of a type of community and have certain rights and obligations within that community. The communitarian claims that what defines communities, nations, and states are the specific interactions and transactions between individuals—caring for a child and being cared for, providing advice and taking advice, leading and being led. The notion of reciprocity between a parent and a child, a minister and a congregation, the president and the people defines socially, morally, and politically who one is and what one owes to others.

A community is the context in which members of a group share common traditions, values, and institutions. Obligations, responsibilities, and rights of members of the community are determined by the web of relationships into which they are born and that they have developed with other members of the community. Conformity to social norms and practices is important in that the adherence to social order perpetuates and preserves the community as a whole. Justice is seen, then, not as an objective, impartial means of deciding restitution but as an interpersonal notion by which members of a community have rights and duties according to the responsibilities they acquire in their relationships to others. This contextual notion of justice, giving each person his or her due, dates back to Aristotle and is known as justice as a kind of proportionate.[21] The individual in the community is seen and judged within the context of his or her status, occupation, and social relationships.

Within these social arrangements, the force and nature of the obligation depends upon how the individual is related to others and, in part, by the social practices and institutions that are agreed upon by the community as a whole. There exists in the community a shared understanding of the impersonal expectations and norms embedded in roles and relationships that qualify all social arrangements. For example, a parent is judged by the duties and responsibilities the community ascribes to the role of parenting. How well you fulfill your responsibilities as a parent is determined in large part by how others in the community perceive you to be fulfilling the duties of a parent. The roles and the relationships and the institutions that are created to buttress them define not only who one is but also whether one is acting justly or unjustly toward others.

The communitarian would find fault with the statist position in two respects. First, the statist position is too simplistic in that it conflates the notion of community with that of statehood. For the communitarian, membership and relationships are the substances that make up the community and the glue that binds it. The institutional structure, such as statehood, is not integral to understanding the essence of the community. Second, the statist position wrongly identifies the state (or the fit between a government and its people) as the seat of political legitimacy.[22] Statehood, for a communitarian, may be a political necessity in order for the community to survive as a whole, but it is neither integral to the identity of the community nor does it define the values and create the institutions of a community. Political legitimacy arises from the common life, the shared historical tradition, practices, and values of a group of people. Without the common life, political institutions as well as the notion of justice have no context, and individuals have no understanding of who they are and what is expected of them.

The difficulty with the communitarian view is that members of a state may engage in a practice, such as slavery, that by another community's standard of justice is considered immoral. According to the communitarian, the political and moral legitimacy of the practice is relative to the accepted norms and practices of the community that engages in slavery. There are no universal grounds for criticizing the community even if one's own society judges it to be morally heinous; because to advocate that a community stop engaging in an unjust practice is also to call for the end to the practice of slavery, a practice which may be embedded in a community's economic, social, and political fabric. This point can also be extended to other practices such as suttee, circumcision, the treatment of children and women in certain societies, infanticide, and abortion. We can extend the list to include activities that are often politically motivated, such as torture, terrorism, genocide, and unrestrained use of force.

The United Nations Declaration of Human Rights, according to the communitarian, would have little significance for a society unless that society professed to hold the same values espoused in the declaration. International cooperation and consensus, within the communitarian view, would only be possible if, normatively speaking, communities shared common values and views of what constitutes the good life. For the communitarian, justice is found within a social context that develops and changes as an organic whole. Justice can never be a purely procedural or formal principle that is imposed upon a community or that is abstractly defined by some external authority.

DISCUSSION QUESTIONS

1. *What is the scope of morality within a communitarian view?*
2. *Do we need to define a constituency (e.g., women) that implicitly or explicitly accepts a community's values before we can determine what is just and unjust behavior?*
3. *What is the basis for a communitarian approach to justice: individuals, the roles they perform, institutions in a society?*

THE COSMOPOLITAN VIEW

According to the cosmopolitan, contemporary events and developments in the world give us good reasons to believe that the nature of domestic affairs has fundamentally changed due to changes in international affairs. Within this viewpoint, the state of international affairs has changed in three ways. First, the nations of the world are increasingly reliant upon one another in terms of trade, finance, and the preservation of the environment. Second, for all intents and purposes, the development of global regulative regimes and institutions such as the World Bank, GATT, United Nations Charter on the Economic Rights and Duties of States and, in particular, the economic multilateral institutions such as the IMF, are "the constitutional structure of the world economy; their activities have important distributive implications."[23] Third, the evolution of international law and the creation of political institutions assist in regulating the global distribution of income and property. Modern states function in a world in which they are no longer "truly self-contained societies."

The cosmopolitan rejects the statist position that the rules of sovereignty and nonintervention in international relations are primary over claims of justice. Because states are not closed, self-sufficient entities, national boundaries are not morally relevant (as for the statist) to the determination of patterns of distribution. Rather, individuals are the seat of moral and political legitimacy. The way in which institutional practices and patterns of distribution effect the freedom and equality of persons, regardless of their nationality, is the basis for justice.

It would be inaccurate to say that the cosmopolitan completely rejects the distinction between a domestic sphere of politics and justice, on the one hand, and an international one, on the other. From a cosmopolitan perspective certain claims to sovereignty still have legitimacy in international relations. Thus, a country can deny assistance to famine stricken peoples in other countries if the aid is being used domestically to create a more just society. When domestic institutions and practices uphold and equally protect the liberties of citizens, then an appeal to sovereignty in order to justify their existence is legitimate.

There are also morally good reasons for disregarding claims of sovereignty and for sanctioning intervention in domestic affairs. Such intervention would bring about changes that would create a more equitable society. Justice applies to one sphere of activity—the international arena—"the entire global scheme of social cooperation."[24]

The just or unjustness of domestic and international practices and institutional patterns of distribution are measured against one standard of justice. Because there is only one standard, nations will be less likely to attempt to act on their own and engage in free-riding.[25] With the existence of one standard of justice that applies to both domestic and international affairs, war would be a means of last resort in an attempt to secure the resources people need in order to provide for their welfare. The redistribution of wealth, technology, and goods from industrialized countries to developing countries is a requirement of justice. Failure to engage in practices of redistribution would mean the perpetuation of unjust international orders and regimes that do not respect peoples' liberties or treat people equally.

The cosmopolitan position asserts that international political and economic processes are not all that different from, and may even be considered an extension of, those conducted within the boundaries of a given state. From this standpoint, states are not self-contained, closed societies. Instead, they are increasingly finding their domestic affairs to be influenced and, in some aspects, directly controlled by outside forces. Given this interdependence, "the world is not, and hardly will be again, one in which a standard of global justice is unnecessary or undemanding."[26]

Institutions that engage in practices that treat people merely as a means to other's ends are morally unjust. The first test to establish whether or not a practice is morally questionable is to determine whether or not people are being used merely as agents to someone else's benefit. For example, deception is a morally questionable practice in that the people who are being deceived are unable to assent (in retrospect) to being treated as a means to someone else's end. In addition, a morally questionable mean, in the cosmopolitan view, is defined as an activity that people would not willingly choose if they had the opportunity to do so. In other words, people would never choose as their own end practices (such as torture) that are demeaning. Nor would they choose to engage in practices (such as economic and trade embargoes) that would directly and significantly harm the quality of life in their country. From the perspective of the recipient government and its people, they would never willingly take on those types of activities that are contrary to their own good.

It is fairly routine in international relations for countries to treat each other merely as means to their own ends. Nations trade with each other without regard for the domestic distribution of goods within a society. In the 1960s, for instance, corporations introduced commercial soybean farming to Brazil. The introduction of this export crop changed Brazilian farming patterns, thereby reducing the availability of staple foods, in particular, the black bean, a principal source of protein in the diet of poor Brazilians. The reduced availability and subsequent rise in price of the black bean meant that more Brazilians would go without a source of protein to the benefit of corporations exporting soybean.

International institutions and regimes also would use methods that treat countries as means to other's ends. This is usually done by imposing economic and trade sanctions and by attaching stringent economic conditions to loans. Unjust activities and patterns in global affairs can only be redressed, according to the cosmopolitan view, by interventionary measures that seek a redistribution of goods in order to make a more just world. Which of these interventionary measures are morally permissible will be gauged by the salient point for the cosmopolitan: Treat people as ends and never as a means.

Even if we agreed with the cosmopolitan that there ought to be one standard of justice for all people, there is no common culture in international affairs that could provide the basis for consensus within the cosmopolitan's view of persons as ends in themselves. Different cultures have different conceptions of human worth. Furthermore, among cultures there exists a diversity of views as to what constitutes the good life. Whose view is to become the universal one? The conception of justice advanced by the cosmopolitan is simply too abstract to provide sufficient content to the list of liberties and goods we need in order to have a global community of humanity that functions with one standard of justice.

Another problem with the cosmopolitan view is that in international relations it is explicitly assumed that the state is the political entity by which the basic liberties and goods of citizens are protected. Although the cosmopolitan may be correct in pointing out that states are not self-contained entities, the state remains the de facto and de jure protector of peoples' liberties and goods. The notion of state sovereignty is the working basis of the United Nations system and other international orders and institutions in international affairs. The question that the cosmopolitan needs to address seriously is, would people be treated more justly if there were a world government and no states?

The cosmopolitan view seeks to reconfigure our thinking about international relations in terms of, first, a community of humanity (people as ends) and, second, an association of states. The cosmopolitan view of justice requires that foreigners intervene in the domestic affairs of another state when people are being treated unjustly; redistribute natural resources in a fair manner among all peoples; and work to make the practices and procedures of international institutions and orders more just. From this standpoint the requirements of justice are quite weighty. They demand a level of moral accountability that, as some detractors have pointed out, may not only be too demanding but may also be counterproductive, creating international political turmoil by condoning too much foreign intervention in the domestic affairs of states.

DISCUSSION QUESTIONS

1. *Within the cosmopolitan view, under what conditions ought a state's sovereignty be respected?*
2. *According to the cosmopolitan view, if outsiders can legitimately interfere in the internal affairs of a state when its citizens are being treated unjustly, then*

on what grounds can outsiders interfere in the domestic affairs of a state when the policies of that state are unjustly discriminating against outsiders?
3. What ends ought to determine an international standard of distributive justice?

NOTES

1. For the ground-breaking article on new definitions of security see Jessica Tuchman Mathews, "Redefining Security," *Foreign Affairs* 68, no. 2 (Spring 1989): 162-177.

2. In using the terms "international order" and "international regime" I am following the distinction made by Oran Young in his book *International Cooperation: Building Regimes for Natural Resources and the Environment* (Ithaca, N.Y.: Cornell University Press, 1989), pp. 12-15.

3. The United Nations Charter states in Article 2(4): "All members [of the United Nations] shall refrain in their international relations from the threat or use of force against the territorial integrity or political independence of any state or in any other manner inconsistent with the purposes of the United Nations."

The Charter of the Organization of American States provides that: "Article 18. No State or group of States has the right to intervene, directly or indirectly, for any reason whatever, in the internal or external affairs of any other State. The foregoing principle prohibits not only armed force but also any other form of interference or attempted threat against the personality of the State or against its political, economic, and cultural elements.

Article 19. No State may use or encourage the use of coercive measures of an economic or political character in order to force the sovereign will of another State and obtain from it advantages of any kind.

Article 20. The territory of a State is inviolable; it may not be the object, even temporarily, of military occupation or of other measures of force taken by another State, directly or indirectly, on any grounds whatever. No territorial acquisitions or special advantages obtained either by force or by other means of coercion shall be recognized."

4. Ralph Pettman, *State and Class: A Sociology of International Affairs* (London: Croom Helm, 1979), pp. 88-95; Robert O. Keohane, *After Hegemony: Cooperation and Discord in the World Political Economy* (Princeton, N.J.: Princeton University Press, 1984), pp. 10-11.

5. World Bank, *Human Development Report 1990* (Oxford: Oxford University Press, 1990), p. 10.

6. See Thomas Hobbes, *Leviathan*. ed. with an introduction by C. B. Macpherson. Part 2 (London: Penguin Books, 1985).

7. *Ibid.*, Part 1, p. 190.

8. See Dennis C. Mueller, *Public Choice* (Cambridge: Cambridge University Press, 1979), pp. 14-18; Mancur Olson, Jr. and Richard Zeckhauser, "An Economic Theory of Alliances," *Review of Economics and Statistics* 48 (1966): 266-279.

9. See World Resources Institute, *World Resources 1990-1991* (Oxford: Oxford University Press, 1990), pp. 135-136. Steven R. Weisman, "Bluefin Tuna and African Elephants Win Some Help at a Global Meeting," *New York Times*, 11 March 1992, p. A8.

10. W. L. La Croix defines intervention as any activity of one state in which it deliberately acts to affect the internal or external affairs of another state in "such a way as to reduce the independence, sovereignty, or self-help qualities of the target state . . . Its essence is to act using some sort of material power, as distinct from moral persuasion, in order to affect what the other state does so that the other state does, in some important area, what the intervening state wants." *War and International Ethics* (Lanham, Md.: University Press of America, 1988), p. 233.

11. This view has been developed by Michael Walzer. See his "The Moral Standing of States: A Response to Four Critics," *in International Ethics*, ed. by Charles Beitz et al. (Princeton, N.J.: Princeton University Press, 1985), pp. 217-237; especially p. 219; pp. 225-226.

12. *Ibid.*, p. 219.

13. *Ibid.*, p. 222.

14. *Ibid.*, pp. 225-227.

15. "Community" in the *Oxford English Dictionary* 2d Edition, ed. James A. H. Murray, Henry Bradley, W.A. Craigic, and C. T. Onions (Oxford: Clarendon Press, 1989), pp. 581-582.

16. *Webster's New World Dictionary* College Edition, ed. David B. Guralink and Joseph H. Friend (Cleveland: The World Publishing Company, 1966), p. 977.

17. "Nation" in the *Oxford English Dictionary*, pp. 231-232.

18. For the information in this paragraph we are indebted to the work of E. J. Hobsbawn, *Nations and Nationalism Since 1780* (Cambridge: Cambridge University Press, 1990), Chapter 1.

19. "State" in the *Oxford English Dictionary*, p. 553.

20. Interpretations of the communitarian position can be found in Eugene Kamenka and Alice E. S. Tay, "The Traditions of Justice," *Law and Philosophy* vol. 5 (1986): 281-313; Michael Sandel, "The Procedural Republic and the Unencumbered Self," *Political Theory* 12 (1984): 81-96; Christina Hoff Sommers, "Filial Morality," *The Journal of Philosophy* 83 (August 1986): 439-456.

21. Aristotle, *Nicomachean Ethics*, ed. and with a translation by Richard McKeon (New York: Random House, 1941), pp. 1,131a3-1,131b20.

22. Michael Walzer, who is the main proponent of the Morality of States position, holds that "the real subject of my argument is not the state at all but the community that (usually) underlies it." Yet, as critics of Walzer's position have pointed out, the domestic contract is between the government and the community. In international relations, the global community is made up of independent states. In his earlier writings, Walzer can be seen as advocating a statist point of view. In his later writings, he develops a communitarian position.

23. Charles R. Beitz, *Political Theory and International Relations* (Princeton, N.J.: Princeton University Press, 1979), p. 148.

24. See *ibid.*, p. 150.

25. The two principles are the Principle of Liberty and the Principle of Equality developed by John Rawls, *A Theory of Justice* (Cambridge, Mass.: Harvard University Press, 1971), pp. 302-303. Charles Beitz applies them to international relations. See his *Political Theory*, pp. 129ff.

26. Thomas Pogge, *Realizing Rawls* (Ithaca, N.Y.: Cornell University Press, 1989), p. 263.

2

"JUST CAUSE"?
THE 1989 U.S. INVASION
OF PANAMA

This case study examines the moral and political legitimacy of the steps that led up to the U.S. invasion of Panama and the moral justness of the invasion itself. Did the United States act appropriately? Did it exhaust all diplomatic means of resolving the conflict before invading? The military invasion was an extreme response on the part of the United States to an increasingly frustrating and embarrassing foreign policy predicament. General Manuel Antonio Noriega's involvement with the Colombian drug cartels was becoming public knowledge, and the U.S. Congress was investigating the corruption of the Panamanian Defense Forces (PDF). In addition, Noriega had assisted Ronald Reagan's administration in its efforts to supply and fund the Contras. Realizing that public knowledge of Noriega's activities was gradually and significantly harming U.S. interests in Central America, officials in George Bush's administration pressured Noriega to step down. Noriega refused.

The invasion achieved what diplomatic means could not, the removal of Noriega from power. Was the invasion justified? The use of military force as

---

This chapter is an edited version of the case study by Christopher Tatham and Rachel McCleary, "Just Cause"? The 1989 United States Invasion of Panama, Pew case study no. 461.

a legitimate means of last resort assumes that every possible means of diplomatic resolution has been exhausted and that the end to be achieved by military force is justified. The Bush administration gave four reasons for the invasion: "to protect American lives, to support democracy, bring fugitive Manuel Antonio Noriega to justice, and protect the integrity of the Panama Canal Treaties." Are these reasons, either individually or collectively, sufficient to justify the military action? Is the goal of the removal of a de facto head of state by another country a politically justified end?

*   *   *

At one o'clock in the morning on 20 December 1989, more than 24,000 U.S. troops invaded the Republic of Panama. The invasion, code named "Operation Just Cause," was the largest combat mission for U.S. soldiers since the Vietnam War. Within hours, U.S. forces secured major Panamanian military installations, the ports of Cristobal and Balboa, Tecumen International Airport and the Bridge of the Americas.[1] By the end of the week, most of the 15,000 members of the Panamanian Defense Forces had surrendered.

On 3 January 1990, Noriega, the principal target of the invasion, turned himself over to U.S. authorities after spending ten days in the residence of Monsignor Sebastian Laboa, the papal nuncio. Noriega's surrender marked the end of more than two decades of military rule in Panama.

In spite of its success, the invasion was devastating for the country of Panama. According to official figures, 516 Panamanians were killed, including 202 civilians. Unofficial estimates place civilian deaths between 202 and 4,000.[2] Several buildings, including ten blocks of mostly wooden houses surrounding the PDF headquarters in Panama City, were destroyed, leaving an estimated 15,000 Panamanians homeless. Altogether the invasion caused more than $1 billion worth of damage.[3]

The destruction accompanying the U.S. invasion has stirred widespread debate regarding its ethical and legal justifications. Supporters argue that military intervention by the United States was the only means of restoring democracy. They cite the long history of U.S. involvement in Panama and the popular support Panamanians gave to the invasion. Opponents, such as the Latin American members of the Organization of American States, contend that the invasion was illegitimate because it violated Panamanian sovereignty. Opponents believe that diplomatic measures could have been taken to resolve the crisis.

This case study asks the student to examine the 1989 U.S. invasion of Panama in terms of both its justness and its legitimacy. Was the invasion another instance of overt U.S. paternalism in Central America? Or did the United States have justified reasons for intervening militarily?

NORIEGA EXPOSED

In June 1987, after Noriega removed him from his position as chief of staff, Colonel Roberto Diaz Herrera publicly denounced the massive corruption within the regime and confirmed public suspicions that Noriega had ordered the 1985 murder of one of his most vociferous critics, Hugo Spadafora.[4]

Diaz Herrera, the cousin of the deceased dictator Omar Torrijos, was due to take command of the PDF that June. Fearing that Diaz Herrera, as PDF commander, would mount a military coup against him, Noriega offered him the ambassadorship to Japan and the position of chief of the Yokohama and Kobe consulates. Diaz Herrera agreed to accept Noriega's offer on the condition that Noriega allow him to keep his military rank. The ambassadorship of Japan, one of the most prestigious positions in the Panamanian foreign service, would have given Diaz Herrera increased influence and wealth. Noriega abruptly reneged on the agreement and retired Diaz Herrera on 2 June without offering him a substitute position.

Angry and fearing that Noriega would arrest him for high treason (punishable by death), Diaz Herrera publicly took the offensive against Noriega. At a press conference on Friday, 5 June 1987, Diaz Herrera admitted that he had carried out Noriega's orders to rig the 1984 Panamanian presidential elections. In the 1984 elections the people of Panama elected Arnulfo Arias president. Noriega declared the election void and named as president his own candidate, Nicolas Ardito Barletta. Panamanians were outraged and openly referred to Barletta as the "Fraudito."[5] The United States did not publicly object to the violation of the electoral process.

Diaz Herrera also told reporters that Noriega was responsible for beheading Hugo Spadafora. Panamanians regarded Spadafora as one of the few Panamanians capable of organizing a violent resistance to the Noriega regime. Diaz Herrera also claimed that Noriega and the Central Intelligence Agency (CIA) jointly planned the airplane crash that killed Omar Torrijos in 1981 and that Noriega personally pocketed $12 million the Shah of Iran gave the Panamanian government in exchange for political refuge.

The public reaction to Diaz Herrera's accusations was one of support and curiosity. A crowd gathered outside his home, and his former detractors visited him in a show of support. Noriega's riot troops, called "Dobermans," attacked the crowd with tear gas and bird shot. Panamanians, not accustomed to open violence, retreated. But the catalyst had occurred.

The accusations made by Diaz Herrera gave life to the opposition group, the Civic Crusade for Justice and Democracy. The Civic Crusade was a coalition of twenty-six civic organizations and representatives from the Catholic church. Upon hearing Diaz Herrera's accusations, these various groups agreed to form an organized opposition to the Noriega regime. Aurelio Barria, the president of the Chamber of Commerce, organized the first meeting and called for peaceful street demonstrations similar to those that toppled the Ferdinand Marcos regime in the Philippines.

For nearly a week, massive demonstrations against Noriega took place in Panama City. Businesses closed and thousands of Panamanians marched in the streets. The demonstrations usually began at lunchtime or before the cocktail hour in the evening. People stood outside apartments and office buildings waving handkerchiefs and beating on pots. Drivers in cars and buses honked their horns.

Despite the relatively peaceful nature of the demonstrations, Noriega's regime declared a state of emergency on 11 June. The Dobermans dispersed the crowds with water canons, tear gas, and by shooting live ammunition into the crowds. Opposition newspapers and television stations were shut down. Hundreds of Panamanians were arrested as the military took control of the streets.

The unrest in Panama occurred at a politically difficult time for the administration of President Ronald Reagan. First, the Iran-Contra affair congressional hearings were being held in the United States. The hearings were investigating the Reagan administration's circumvention of congressional restrictions on funding of the Nicaraguan covert armed group known as the Contras. Second, the effectiveness of the Reagan administration's "War on Drugs," spearheaded by the Drug Enforcement Agency (DEA), was being questioned. Illegal narcotics traffic from Latin America to the United States was continuing to rise as the government allocated less funds for drug interdiction. Third, the political unrest in Panama was jeopardizing plans to transfer majority control of the canal to Panama in 1990. The Panama Canal Commission, with a total of nine representatives from both Panama and the United States, was working out the details for the transfer of control. The commission, an independent agency that regulates the canal, was due to change membership from a U.S. majority to a Panamanian majority of five members, one of whom would become chair.

The CIA and Noriega

Noriega had assumed a critical role in each of the three affairs. Through his political connections with Latin American leaders and senior officials in the U.S. government, Noriega had become and had continued as an important informant and confidant to several U.S. agencies for nearly thirty years. In 1960, while he was a student at a Peruvian military academy, the CIA recruited Noriega to collect minor intelligence information on other students.[6] In 1970, after he had risen to chief of Panamanian intelligence

(G-2), Noriega began giving the CIA information about leaders and leftist movements in Latin America. Through his mentor, dictator Omar Torrijos, Noriega developed a personal relationship with Cuban leader Fidel Castro. As his power grew, Noriega assisted the Cuban government in obtaining U.S. technology by allowing the Cubans to purchase goods from the Colón free trade zone in Panama.

Noriega was also a "strategic asset" to the Pentagon and for William Casey, director of the CIA. Noriega supplied the United States with information on Cuban activities in Central America, and he assisted the U.S. efforts to support the Contras. The Contras were a CIA-created insurgency group originally consisting of former members of the late Nicaraguan dictator Anastasio Somoza Debayle's National Guard. In 1981, the CIA merged the group with a small counterrevolutionary group, forming the Nicaraguan Democratic Force. Casey, who used covert operations as a routine CIA instrument for carrying out the Reagan administration's foreign policy, personally visited Noriega to drum up support for the Contras. Through Casey, Noriega began to assist the CIA in its efforts to fund and arm the Contras. In addition to some financial support, Noriega gave the CIA access to planes and airfields.[7]

The Reagan Administration and Noriega

The Boland amendment, passed by Congress in October 1984, legally put the CIA arms pipeline to the Contras out of business. The Reagan administration's man in charge of circumventing the congressional restrictions was Lt. Col. Oliver North. That same year, to obtain Noriega's support for the Contras, William Casey flew to Panama with North to visit Noriega.[8] After that, North became the Reagan administration's contact person on the Contras to Noriega. During three visits to Panama, North developed a working relationship with Noriega. On 17 January 1985, North accompanied National Security Council chief, Robert McFarlane, to discuss "options for support to the armed/unarmed opposition" to the Nicaraguan government. The idea was to obtain Central American support in the form of "lethal assistance" for the Contras, something the Reagan administration was forbidden to do under the Boland amendment.

In June, North met with Noriega to discuss the training of potential Contra leaders. Noriega agreed to set up a training program in Panama for them. In October, Noriega asked North to make an unscheduled stopover in Panama. Noriega was having difficulty renegotiating an agreement with the International Monetary Fund and the World Bank. He asked North to press Panama's case with those in the Reagan administration who could assist Panama in obtaining financial assistance.

As a result of these meetings between North and Noriega, Panama assumed a more significant role in operations dealing with Iran and the Contras known as "The Enterprise." In close coordination with Iranian-born businessman Albert Hakim and Richard Secord, a former U.S. general, North set up secret Panamanian corporations, such as Lake Resources and Stanford Technology. These were fronts to hide North's funneling of money from Iranian arms sales to the Contras. Other companies, Udall and NRAF Inc., were fronts for the Contra arms supply operation. Money to the Nicaraguan Democratic Force was transferred from these fictitious companies to Contra accounts through Panamanian banks. Noriega's cooperation was needed to keep the transfers concealed.

Noriega provided assistance to the CIA through his political adviser Michael Harari, who channeled arms from Israel and Soviet-bloc countries to the Contras. Harari, the Israeli ex officio representative for Israeli operations in Panama, mediated Israeli assistance and equipped the G-2 with sophisticated espionage and surveillance techniques. Harari made contacts through CIA Latin American directorate chief, Dewey Claridge, and President Bush's National Security adviser Donald Gregg to establish a network of airfields and support for the Contras. Through Harari, Noriega offered the CIA landing rights at three different airstrips in Panama: Chiriqui province, Veraguas province, and Patilla Airport.

In October 1985, Casey personally lobbied to defeat an amendment that would require the CIA to release incriminating evidence on Noriega. The amendment required the CIA to report to the U.S. House and Senate Intelligence Committees on the charges of the Panamanian Defense Forces' involvement in drugs, arms trafficking, money laundering, and the death of Hugo Spadafora.

The Medellín Cartel and Noriega

Pressure from Casey to conceal Noriega's involvement in covert CIA activities was countered by pressure from officials in the DEA who wanted to bring Noriega to trial. In 1971, the predecessor to the DEA, the Bureau of Narcotics and Dangerous Drugs, set up an office in Panama and began collecting information on prominent Panamanians involved in drug trafficking. One of the people on the list was Lieutenant Colonel Noriega who, as chief of Panamanian intelligence, was in a position to personally control and benefit from the drug traffic in the country. Initially, Noriega allowed the Medellín cartel to use Panama as a transshipment point for Colombian cocaine destined for the United States In late 1983, the cartel paid high-ranking PDF officers approximately $5 million to let it set up a large cocaine lab in the Darién jungle. In 1984, after the assassination of Colombia's justice minister

Rodrigo Lara Bonilla by members of the cartel, Noriega granted leaders of the cartel temporary asylum in Panama.[9]

Although Noriega was one of the DEA's targets in Latin America, he was also one of its strategic assets. For two decades, Noriega assisted the DEA in its efforts against the Colombian cartels. In 1984, Noriega personally gave the United States permission to militarily raid the Colombian-run cocaine operation in Darién. The raid resulted in the confiscation of the largest cache of cocaine precursor chemicals in history (six thousand 55-gallon drums).[10] (It is believed that Noreiga permitted the raid on the lab as a means of pressuring the members of the cartel to reach an agreement with the Colombian government.)

Noriega was in Europe at the time of the raid. Fearing for his life, Noriega flew to Havana to ask Fidel Castro to mediate on his behalf with the cartel. Castro mediated an agreement between Noriega and the cartel. Noriega released twenty-three Colombians arrested in the raid. He returned some of the confiscated lab equipment and $3 million in cash.

DEA attempts to link Noriega to drug trafficking were unsuccessful. Noriega distanced himself from the illegal activities by creating a network of emissaries to conduct negotiations with the Colombian drug cartels and to transport narcotics for him. The break for DEA officials came when two of Noriega's representatives, Steve Kalish and Floyd Carlton, were arrested on drug-related charges.[11] Kalish, a U.S. citizen living in Panama City who had been convicted of marijuana smuggling by a Texas court, served as a liaison between the Colombian drug cartels and General Noriega in 1983-1984. After the Darién drug raid, Kalish helped obtain the release of captured Colombians and assisted in mediating the new rules for the cartel's money-laundering operations in Panama. In 1983, Kalish moved to Panama where the banks could launder the amount of money he earned from marijuana smuggling, sometimes as much as $35 million at a time. Kalish met Noriega through his friendship with Noriega's personal pilot, Caesar Rodriguez. Rodriguez passed on to Kalish U.S. intelligence information collected by the G-2 on drug trafficking activity in Panama. Through Rodriguez and his personal association with Noriega, Kalish eventually gained influence with the dictator.

In July 1984, Kalish was arrested in Tampa, Florida, on drug trafficking charges as he was about to board his Lear jet for a flight back to Panama. He spent the next two years in a prison in Florida. In 1986, the state of Florida increased the charges against Kalish to a penalty of life in prison. Fearing a life sentence, Kalish offered to provide information implicating Noriega in drug-trafficking activities in exchange for reduced charges. For unexplained reasons, the Florida court refused the offer.

Carlton, a pilot who flew drugs to Panama for Colombian drug cartels, was arrested in June 1986 in a U.S. sting operation in Costa Rica. Carlton had originally worked for Noriega in 1978 and 1979 as his personal pilot. Under Noriega's directive, he and a fellow pilot, Caesar Rodriguez, flew supplies to the Nicaraguan Sandinistas in Costa Rica. Rodriguez was murdered in March 1986. Carlton suspected that Noriega had ordered the killing to conceal Noriega's involvement in Spadafora's murder. Carlton and Rodriguez were friends of Spadafora at the time of his disappearance and decapitation. Fearing for his own life, Carlton fled to San Jose, Costa Rica, where he was arrested by DEA agents and extradited on drug-trafficking charges.

The DEA, having gathered information from many sources including Carlton and Kalish, was divided on what to do about Noriega. Some DEA officials feared that the War on Drugs would suffer a major setback if charges were not brought against Noriega. Other DEA officials argued that Noriega could continue to be used as an effective tool against the Colombian drug cartels. Casey, director of the CIA, who had personally sought to keep Noriega's association with the CIA efforts to support the Contras out of the Iran-Contra congressional hearings, died in May 1987.

DISCUSSION QUESTIONS

1. *Should the United States be concerned if a leader of another country engages in drug-trafficking, arms selling, and espionage as long as he or she is useful to the United States in meeting foreign policy objectives?*
2. *What constraints ought the citizenry of a country place on the means used by its government in pursuing national interest? What level of accountability should citizens expect from their officials and the agencies they run, for example, William Casey and the CIA?*
3. *There were critical moments when the United States could have acted diplomatically and publicly to support democracy in Panama. What were they? Should the United States have interfered, for ethical and/or pragmatic reasons, at these critical moments to support the Panamanian people in their efforts to remain a democracy?*

THE UNITED STATES REACTS TO PANAMANIAN UNREST

Fearing that domestic unrest in Panama might lead to violence against U.S. citizens living within the former Canal Zone, Panama City, and Colón, the State Department voiced its disapproval of the state of emergency declared by Panamanian authorities on 11 June 1987. More importantly, the Reagan administration feared that civil unrest would destabilize the negotiations taking place on the transfer of power over the Panama Canal. State Department officials, including U.S. Ambassador to Panama Arthur Davis,

met with both Panamanian President Eric Delvalle and General Noriega.
(Barletta resigned in 1985 as president, and Delvalle, his vice president succeeded him.) Assistant Secretary of State for Inter-American Affairs Elliot
Abrams assured the Panamanian leaders that a rift between the United States
and Panama was not desired, but he insisted that the United States was
committed to protecting its interests in the region.

On 26 June, the U.S. Senate, by a vote of 84-2, passed Resolution 239
demanding the restoration of democracy in Panama and the removal of
Noriega while the formal charges of murder and electoral fraud brought
against him were being investigated as a result of Diaz Herrera's
accusations.[12]

Noriega Tightens His Grip

In response to the resolution and fearing the United States would increase
pressure for his resignation, Noriega's regime officially lifted the state of
emergency. Unofficially, Noriega and his supporters organized civil protests
against the United States. On 30 June, 5,000 progovernment demonstrators
marched down the Avenida Balboa and attacked the U.S. Embassy, throwing
stones and smashing cars in the parking lot. Noriega used the orchestrated
attack on the Embassy to show domestic support for his regime in the midst
of rising U.S. pressure. At public rallies, he accused the United States of
seeking to renege on the 1977 Canal Treaties that would give Panamanians
control of the Panama Canal in the year 2000. The combination of the Senate
Resolution, Noriega's anti-American political accusations, and the attack on
the U.S. Embassy in Panama generated considerable media attention and
forced the United States to take some kind of action.

Pressuring Noriega to Step Down

Noriega's relationship with officials in the CIA and the DEA as an informant required Abrams to seek the removal of Noriega from power while
protecting U.S. citizens in Panama without threatening other U.S. interests.
Traditional diplomatic options were not practical alternatives because,
although Noriega ruled the country, President Eric Delvalle was technically
head of state. State Department officials knew that economic sanctions, for
example, would be interpreted by the international community as an attack
against the Delvalle government rather than Noriega. This would bolster both
regional and domestic support for Panama and validate Noriega's claim that
the United States intended to renege on the 1977 Canal Treaties.

Abrams attempted to depoliticize the crisis by focusing on the drug charges against Noriega rather than on political issues. By implicating Noriega in international drug trafficking, the State Department hoped to maintain international support for U.S. efforts to remove Noriega and assist Panamanian domestic opposition groups. Senior officials from the State, Defense, and Justice departments, the CIA, and the DEA met to discuss the option of pursuing drug charges against Noriega. They agreed to allow federal prosecutors in Miami and Tampa, Dick Gregorie and Leon Kellner, respectively, to file charges in U.S. courts. By allowing a lower-level agency to pursue the charges independently, senior-level State Department officials hoped to defuse the crisis and legitimize U.S. attempts to remove Noriega.

In July 1987, Steven Kalish and Floyd Carlton, associates of Noriega, formally provided testimony to prosecutors about Noriega's role in drug trafficking. Although their testimony was not enough to incriminate Noriega, it provided enough information about dates and the location of incriminating evidence for the Florida attorneys to build a credible case against him.

On 5 February 1988, prosecutors in Tampa and Miami announced separate indictments against Noriega (see Table 2.1).

Negotiating the Removal of Noriega

The June uprisings had isolated Panamanian President Eric Delvalle from both his civilian and his military supporters, prompting many of his civilian friends and business associates to join the Civic Crusade. Delvalle refused to launch an extensive investigation into the charges made by Diaz Herrera against Noriega to force Noriega to step down because such an investigation was likely to expose his own participation in the fraudulent 1984 elections and the illegal payoffs he had received from Noriega. Instead, he offered to open a dialogue with the opposition, and he ordered the attorney general to initiate a limited inquiry into the charges surrounding Spadafora's murder.

Although leaders in the Civic Crusade interpreted Delvalle's actions as a sign of support for Noriega, Noriega questioned Delvalle's loyalty. Delvalle had not publicly supported the military crackdown, and his daughter had recently married the brother of opposition leader Roberto Eisenmann, the editor of a newspaper expressing strong anti-Noriega views. Fearing that Delvalle would give in to pressure from his friends in the Civic Crusade, Noriega plotted to remove him from the presidency.

Alienated from both Noriega and the Civic Crusade, Delvalle turned to the United States for support. Because both the State and Justice departments wanted to remove Noriega, U.S. officials were eager to assist Delvalle. By offering his support, Delvalle gave Secretary of State George Shultz the

TABLE 2.1 The Indictments Against General Manuel Antonio Noriega

General Manuel Noriega was indicted on eleven counts of conspiracy, racketeering, importing drugs, traveling to further the conspiracy, and sheltering Colombian cocaine bosses after a political assassination. Noriega is the first foreign leader outside U.S. jurisdiction to be indicted in U.S. federal courts. One minor charge was later dropped.

In the Miami court, Noriega was indicted on the following charges:
1. In return for sheltering Colombia's Medellín drug cartel bosses, Noriega is charged with accepting a minimum payment of $4.6 million.
2. Smugglers were allowed to use Panama as a midpoint for drug shipments from Colombia to the United States.
3. He traveled to Havana, Cuba, to allow President Fidel Castro to mediate a dispute with the Medellín drug cartel after Panamanian troops led the DEA to a Colombian cocaine lab in the Panamanian Darién jungle.
4. He used his position as de facto head of state to provide protection for international narcotics dealers.
5. He arranged for the shipment of chemicals, including those seized by the Panamanian police, used in processing cocaine.
6. He approved the laundering of cartel narcotics money in Panamanian banks.
7. He allowed Medellín cartel operators to shift their operations to Panamanian territory to escape a crackdown in Colombia after the assassination of the minister of justice.

Three charges were filed against Noriega in the Tampa court:
1. Conspiring to import and distribute marijuana.
2. Trying to import more than 1.4 million pounds of marijuana.
3. Accepting a $1 million bribe from Colombian drug dealers so that they could smuggle drugs and launder cash in Panama.

opportunity he needed to politically force Noriega from power. Shultz had been unwilling to embrace opposition leaders in the Civic Crusade because many of its leaders had supported Arnulfo Arias in the 1984 presidential elections. Arias had opposed the U.S. presence in Panama, and Shultz feared that his followers in the Civic Crusade would embrace Arias's nationalistic ideals. By giving support to Delvalle rather than to the Civic Crusade, Shultz avoided potential conflicts with opposition leaders over the U.S. military presence in Panama and the 1977 Canal Treaties.

In the fall of 1987, one of Delvalle's closest advisers, Jose Blandon, the Panamanian consul in New York, arranged for Delvalle to meet with Deputy Assistant Secretary of State William Walker to discuss a plan, later called the "Blandon Plan," to remove Noriega from power. Blandon proposed to Walker that the United States agree to drop the charges against Noriega if Noriega agreed to resign as chief of the Defense Forces. Blandon told Walker that he had formulated the plan after consulting with Delvalle, Noriega, and leaders of the Civic Crusade. But Blandon overstated the success of his meeting with Noriega. He failed to tell Walker that Noriega said he would agree to resign only if he was not forced to remove himself from Panamanian politics. On 20 December, Noriega's intelligence sources in Washington informed him that Blandon had failed to mention Noriega's stipulation. Noriega promptly fired Blandon and advised the State Department that the plan was dead. Although Blandon's plan failed, it became a guide for State Department policy in 1988.

In January 1988, before a Senate Foreign Relations Committee hearing, Blandon testified at length regarding Noriega's involvement with drug trafficking.[13] Blandon linked Noriega with the Colombian drug cartels. On 1 February 1988, Ambassador Arthur Davis met with Delvalle to discuss the impending indictments by two Florida grand juries. After the June 1987 uprisings, Noriega and the Civic Crusade had shunned Delvalle, isolating him from the daily responsibilities of running the country. The United States had become his only source of political and economic support. Delvalle, increasingly isolated, agreed to support the State and Justice departments' plan to indict Noriega.

In late February, Assistant Secretary of State Abrams notified Delvalle about the modified Blandon Plan. Abrams told him that the prosecuting attorneys and the DEA had formulated a deal with the Justice Department to drop the charges against Noriega if Noriega agreed to resign. Delvalle was instructed to use his constitutional power as president to fire Noriega if he refused to accept the offer. Abrams assured Delvalle that the United States would support him regardless of Noriega's decision.

On 25 February, Delvalle publicly dismissed Noriega during a prerecorded television address. Delvalle named Colonel Justine Marcos as Noriega's successor in an attempt to divide Noriega's loyalty among members of the PDF. He also called for public demonstrations to counter Noriega's influence in the National Assembly. Delvalle feared Noriega would coerce legislators in the National Assembly to call for his own resignation. Delvalle hoped public demonstrations would make Noriega think twice before tampering with the nation's only representative body.

Despite the legal justification for Delvalle's move, the plan backfired. Marcos was indicted along with Noriega by the Florida grand jury, and he immediately pledged his allegiance to the general. As Delvalle had predicted,

Noriega called on his political connections in the National Assembly to remove Delvalle from office. Delvalle and his supporters were forced into exile, but they insisted they were the nation's legitimate leaders. Although the United Nations and the Organization of American States received Noriega's newly appointed ambassadors and recognized his hand-picked successor for president, Manuel Solis de Palma, the United States did not. The State Department continued to recognize the exiled government of Eric Delvalle and his designated ambassador to the United States, Juan Sosa.

Imposing Sanctions

The grand jury indictment gave the State Department a political rationale for implementing economic sanctions against Panama. In March, President Reagan used his authority under the International Emergency Economic Powers Act to issue an executive order prohibiting trade and economic transactions with Panama. The order froze all assets of the Panamanian government in the United States with the exception of some authorizations by the exiled president Delvalle. Lease payments to the Panamanian government for U.S. bases in Panama were suspended, and payments by individuals and organizations in the United States to the Noriega regime were banned.

The sanctions had a crippling effect on the Panamanian economy. By curtailing all payments to the country, the Reagan administration effectively froze the Panamanian money supply. As a consequence, the Panamanian government was forced to close the nation's banks for nearly two months. When the banks reopened on 17 April, domestic and foreign companies transferred capital to the United States. Between March 1988 and December 1989, bank deposits dropped by nearly 70 percent. Unemployment increased to more than 30 percent. Gross domestic product (GDP) fell by 20 percent, and the Noriega regime was unable to pay government workers. Members of the Civic Crusade organized demonstrations against the military in response to the economic hardships caused by the sanctions.

The military reacted to the uprisings with force. Noriega organized a personal army within the military called the Dignity Battalions. These soldiers, who placed loyalty to Noriega above loyalty to the nation, were used by Noriega to physically harass his opposition. The military frequently broke up demonstrations with gunfire. An international delegation of physicians, "Physicians for Human Freedom," reported that more than 1,000 Panamanians were injured with bird shot during demonstrations against the military. Radio and television announcers, such as Miguel Antonio Bernal, were physically attacked by the military. The leadership in the National Assembly of Magistrates, union representatives, and cabinet ministers were physically threatened if they attempted to challenge Noriega. Independent newspapers and radio and television stations were shut down if they protested or criticized actions taken by the military.

DISCUSSION QUESTIONS

1. *To what extent did the United States contribute to its own failure in achieving a diplomatic resolution to the Panamanian crisis?*
2. *What kind of obligation, if any, did the United States have to support the only organized domestic opposition, the Civic Crusade?*
3. *The United States employed various diplomatic and economic means to pressure Noriega to step down as the leader of Panama and to maintain democracy in Panama. What legal and moral considerations ought to delimit the kinds of means a foreign power uses to intervene in the internal affairs of another state?*
4. *Did the economic and trade sanctions come at the right time? Whom did they effect? Were they morally legitimate forms of intervention in the internal affairs of Panama? Were they proportionate to the ends to be attained? Was there a probability of success in attaining the desired ends by implementing the sanctions?*

THE UNITED STATES AND MILITARY INTERVENTION

Between March 1988 and May 1989 the State Department could do little but wait to see how the economic sanctions would effect Panama. This period marked a transition in the political leadership of the United States from President Reagan to President George Bush. Presidential elections were to take place in November 1988, and Bush strategists advised him that further negotiations with Noriega risked public accusations of dealing with "a drug dictator."

In May, the Reagan administration sent Michael Kozak, a State Department official, to negotiate Noriega's removal. Kozak was instructed to inform Noriega that if he stepped down, the drug charges against him would be dropped and he would not have to leave Panama. Upon finding out about the conditions presented by Kozak to Noriega, Vice President Bush erupted in rage and sent Kozak back with an ultimatum that Noriega resign by 25 May.[14] Without a credible military invasion to back up the ultimatum, Noriega did not take the message seriously. A military invasion was not politically feasible for Bush because it would most likely alarm voters and be publicly condemned by Central American leaders.

Despite the severity of the economic sanctions, Noriega maintained his grip on power. The military was instrumental in his success. The military allowed him to control the visible positions of leadership in the country through force and bribes. By controlling these positions, Noriega was able to project an image of popular support and maintain his effectiveness in international affairs.

The May 1989 Elections

By 1989, the State Department's plan to use economic sanctions to force Noriega to step down had reached a dead end. The economic sanctions had failed to remove Noriega, and exiled Panamanian President Eric Delvalle's term, now being filled by Noriega's appointed president, Solis de Palma, was coming to a close. The winner of the May election was to replace Delvalle (and Solis de Palma) as president in September. The deadline forced the Bush administration to abandon the Reagan administration's goal of reinstating Delvalle's government in favor of giving support to Civic Crusade leaders in the May elections.

The State Department donated $10 million to support the Civic Crusade against Noriega's presidential candidate and business partner, Carlos Duque. Representatives from most Panamanian political parties opposed to Noriega had joined the Civic Crusade by January 1989. Together, they selected Guillermo Endara, a member of the Arnulfista party, as the opposition candidate for president. Endara's party was not the strongest in Panama, but he was well liked by Panamanians and other party leaders. His selection as a candidate for president eased tensions between the nation's two most powerful political groups, the Christian Democrats and the MOLINERA parties, led by Roberto Arias Calderon and Guillermo "Billy" Ford, respectively. Calderon and Ford agreed to set aside their political differences and run as first and second vice presidential candidates to unify the opposition party against Noriega.

All three candidates threatened Noriega. Each was popular and able to initiate massive demonstrations against the dictator. To counter their popularity, Noriega planned to fix the election. He ordered soldiers to collect ballots, and he reorganized electoral districts to make it difficult for Panamanians to vote. By placing the military in charge of the election, Noriega intended to prevent international observers from maintaining an accurate count of election returns. Noriega was certain that his candidate Carlos Duque would win.

Noriega underestimated public support for the opposition. Unofficial election results from the 7 May elections indicated that, in spite of Noriega's interference, Guillermo Endara won by more than a three-to-one margin.

The election results were confirmed by international observers, including former U.S. Presidents Jimmy Carter and Gerald Ford. When it was clear that his candidate had been defeated, Noriega nullified the results, calling them a fraud. Noriega then directed the National Assembly to confirm his long-time friend, Francisco Rodriguez, as the president of Panama. Rodriguez remained president of Panama until the United States invasion.

To show opposition to Noriega's decision to annul the election, thousands of Panamanians flooded the streets waving handkerchiefs and banging pots. Noriega responded with another violent crackdown. On 10 May, Guillermo Endara and Guillermo Ford were beaten by members of Noriega's Dignity Battalions in the middle of a busy street in downtown Panama City. The strategic violence, against two such visible public figures, was effective in intimidating Panamanians. Photos of the beatings in U.S. newspapers and on television generated public support for the Bush administration's decision to recognize Endara's government as the legitimate government of Panama.

Many Panamanians began to expect the United States to take direct action against Noriega. The United States had intervened previously dozen of times, militarily and politically, in Panama. They thought the United States would do the same now to oust Noriega. Despite widespread opposition to the Noriega regime, the military remained firmly in control of the government. Efforts by groups like the Civic Crusade helped to delegitimize the military regime, but they were unable to directly challenge Noriega's military or economic power.

President Bush, who had been highly criticized in the U.S. press for not taking action in the Panamanian crisis, dispatched 1,882 marines in response to the uprisings and threats by Panamanian soldiers against U.S. citizens in Panama.

The U.S. Military Option Becomes a Reality

In February 1988, Secretary of State George Shultz publicly appealed to PDF officers to mount a coup against Noriega. Shultz told them that Noriega was the cause of hostility between the United States and Panama and stressed that Noriega's removal would lead to the restoration of harmonious relations with PDF leaders and the United States. On 16 March 1988, a few air force officers and the head of the PDF's police division, Colonel Leonidas Macias, responded to the plea by attempting to mount a coup, but soldiers loyal to Noriega suppressed it. In response to the coup attempt and to a general strike spreading throughout the country, Noriega reorganized the military forces. He dismissed 18 officers and promoted 104 officers. In promoting the officers, Noriega placed his favorite officers over those who had seniority in the system.

By the end of March, Noriega had acquired enough currency to meet some of the government's payrolls. The cash had come from taxes paid by U.S. companies with offices in Panama and from Panamanian assets in the Latin American Export Bank that had been converted into hard currency in Europe.

As economic pressure failed to remove Noriega from power, Latin American leaders began to publicly condemn the sanctions. On 29 March, at the Latin American Economic System meeting, twenty-two countries urged the Reagan administration to remove the sanctions. The group publicly stated that it would consider a request by Panama for economic assistance. The president of Mexico, expressing a popular Latin American view, stated that the United States was interfering "in political matters that are the sole concern of the Panamanian people."

In July, President Bush ordered the U.S. Southern Command (Southcom) to relocate 2,160 service members and their dependents in Panama from off-base housing to military installations. Although the move was primarily intended as a psychological threat to Noriega, it introduced military action as an option. Operations were staged along the canal and a helicopter-borne assault was staged to show that U.S. forces could protect and evacuate the U.S. Embassy complex in downtown Panama City. One of the purposes for staging the operations was to goad the Panamanian Defense Forces into attacking. But it did not happen.

Seeking a "Latin American" solution to the mounting crisis, President Bush supported an Organization of American States effort to mediate a peaceful transition. Noriega scheduled meetings with the OAS delegation where U.S. military operations were taking place. He would cancel other meetings, citing U.S. interference in the internal affairs of Panama. The OAS delegation finally succeeded in brokering a deal between the Panamanian opposition and Noriega's representative. The agreement involved Noriega's resignation and new presidential elections. Upon public disclosure of the agreement, Noriega refused to accept it and denounced his representative for exceeding his authority.

In September, a Miami lawyer representing Noriega called Michael Kozak at the State Department. The lawyer stated that Noriega wished to initiate talks with the Reagan administration as the economic sanctions were only hurting Panama and there was no movement toward a resolution. At the same time this proposal was made, Major Moises Giroldi, the Panamanian officer who had put down the March 1988 coup, approached CIA agents with a plan to unseat Noriega. Giroldi was one of Noriega's most trusted military officers. After the attempted coup in 1988, Noriega had promoted Giroldi and made him chief of the security forces. Through his new position, Giroldi developed a loyal following in the PDF, one capable of challenging the dictator.

The October 1989 Coup Attempt

Giroldi told CIA agents that he was dissatisfied with Noriega's handling of the crisis. He feared the general's actions would lead to armed conflict with U.S. soldiers in Panama. Giroldi explained that his supporters could capture Noriega and take command of his soldiers at the PDF headquarters in Panama City. He needed U.S. troops to prevent reinforcements at nearby installations from rescuing Noriega. This could be accomplished if U.S. soldiers blocked three major roads leading to the headquarters.

Giroldi's plan represented what officials in the State Department had wanted: a Panamanian solution to the crisis, with limited U.S. involvement. Despite the apparent simplicity of the plan, it failed as the result of misunderstandings, hidden agendas, and suspicion among U.S. officials and the coup's leader.

From the beginning, communication between U.S. agents and Giroldi was a problem. During their first meeting with Giroldi, CIA agents listened to his plan but did not outright promise him U.S. assistance. Unlike William Casey, who had strongly supported covert activities, the new CIA director, Judge William Webster, ran operations strictly by the book. Webster took over in the wake of the Iran-Contra scandal. The Senate Intelligence Committee had placed restrictions on CIA involvement in coup attempts against Noriega. Webster did not want to back any efforts that could be construed as illegal assistance from the CIA. Although the CIA agents did not promise U.S. assistance, they did not refuse either. They told Giroldi that new regulations prevented them from being specific about U.S. support and that they were not permitted to maintain direct contact with anyone planning a coup against the dictator. Before leaving, however, they assured Giroldi that they would consider his plan. Giroldi interpreted this response as a subtle indication of their willingness to help.

On 1 October, just two days before the coup was scheduled to occur, General Maxwell Thurman replaced General Frederick Woerner as head of U.S. military operations in Panama. Bush was dissatisfied with Woerner's persistent comments downgrading the effectiveness of U.S. foreign policy in Panama. Unlike Woerner, Thurman did not publicly comment on policy issues. Nicknamed "Mad Max," Thurman was one of the Pentagon's most experienced combat leaders. During the summer of 1989, Woerner's staff had developed contingency plans to remove Noriega by military force. Bush wanted Thurman in Panama if he decided to use them.

Thurman was suspicious of the coup from the beginning. Giroldi had been one of Noriega's most loyal officers, and intelligence reports suggested that Noriega might have fabricated the entire plan. Noriega was a master of counterintelligence, and U.S. agents in Panama were unable to verify the reliability of their sources. Noriega had made the United States look foolish before, and Thurman suspected he was about to do so again.

Inaccurate intelligence information, coupled with the CIA's reluctance to directly participate in the coup, prevented information about Giroldi's plan from reaching senior U.S. officials in Washington until 2 October. President Bush met with Secretary of Defense Richard Cheney, Secretary of State James Baker, National Security Adviser Brent Scowcroft, Chief of Staff General Colin Powell, and Vice President Dan Quayle. None of them was well informed about the coup. CIA director William Webster was out of town. Like Thurman, Cheney suspected that Giroldi was still loyal to Noriega. Baker was concerned about the legal ramifications. If Noriega were killed in the coup, the United States could be accused of plotting to assassinate a world leader, a violation of international law, congressional restrictions, and an executive order. None of the officials knew much about Giroldi, and all were concerned about his commitment to democracy. The United States had supported President Guillermo Endara since the May 1989 elections, and Bush had pledged to support democracy in Panama. Not knowing the nature of Giroldi's political allegiances, Bush postponed making a decision to give U.S. support to the coup. By the time he learned of Giroldi's intentions, the coup would be over.

Given little guidance from Washington, Thurman chose to put U.S. forces on alert. He informed Noriega (as was required by the 1977 treaties) that the United States would be conducting routine military exercises as they had done many times before the coup. Thurman ordered U.S. troops to block two of the three avenues requested by Giroldi until additional orders came from Washington.

Giroldi interpreted the exercises as a signal that the United States had decided to support the coup. He proceeded as planned, unaware of Bush's stipulation requiring a confirmation of his commitment to democracy. After capturing Noriega, Giroldi's soldiers waited for U.S. troops to move into position, but they never did. Thurman was not given orders to act, and Noriega's reinforcements arrived at the PDF headquarters unimpeded, via the one avenue not blocked by U.S. troops. Noriega was freed. Most of the rebels, including Giroldi, were tortured and executed.

Last Ditch Effort

With the coup attempt a failure, the Bush administration sought one more time to negotiate with Noriega. On 12 October, the United States presented Noriega with the following condition for his resignation. If he resigned, the United States would not extradite him to stand trial on drug charges, but the drug charges would not be dropped. Kozak was sent to Panama to ask Noriega to make a specific proposal in response to the U.S. condition. Noriega said he would consider the condition.

TABLE 2.2   Resolution of the Organization of American States

The following resolution, #534 (800/89),
was adopted by the Organization of
American States on 22 December 1989.

Serious Events in the Republic of Panama

THE PERMANENT COUNCIL OF THE ORGANIZATION OF AMERICAN STATES HAVING SEEN:

The serious events in the Republic of Panama, especially the armed clashes resulting from the military intervention by the United States and the deplorable loss of lives and property;

The obligation of States not to intervene, directly or indirectly, for any reason whatever, in the internal or external affairs of any other State, and

The obligation to respect the inviolability of the territory of a State, which may not be the object, even temporarily, of military occupation or of other measures of force taken by another State, directly or indirectly, on any grounds whatever, and

CONSIDERING:

The provisions of resolution I adopted by the Twenty-first Meeting of Consultation of Ministers of Foreign Affairs on May 17, 1989 and the declarations made by the President of the Meeting and adopted on June 6, July 20, and August 24, 1989 on the Panamanian crisis in its international context;

That, at its nineteenth regular session, the General Assembly requested the Permanent Council to keep the situation in Panama under permanent consideration;

That any just and lasting solution to the Panamanian problem must be based upon full respect for the right of its people to self-determination without outside interference;

That it is necessary to guarantee full respect for the sovereignty of Panama;

That it is also necessary to reestablish conditions that will guarantee the full exercise of the human rights and fundamental freedoms of the Panamanian people;

That the Panamanian people have the unalienable right to self-determination without internal dictates or external influence,

RESOLVES:

1. To deeply regret the military intervention in Panama.

2. To urge the immediate cessation of hostilities and bloodshed and to request the launching of negotiations between the various political sectors of

the country that will lead to a concerted solution to the Panamanian institutional crisis.

3. To express its deepest concern over the serious incidents and the loss of lives taking place in the Republic of Panama.

4. To call for the withdrawal of the foreign troops used for the military intervention and to reaffirm that solving the crisis Panama is undergoing at this time necessarily requires full respect for the right of the Panamanian people to self-determination without outside interference and faithful adherence to the letter and spirit of the Torrijos-Carter treaties.

5. To express the need to comply with the obligations assumed by the States in the Vienna Conventions on Diplomatic and Consular Relations.

6. To urge that the International Committee of the Red Cross (ICRC) be provided with the facilities and cooperation necessary for it to carry out its humanitarian work with the wounded and the civilian population.

7. To express its fraternal support for and solidarity with the Panamanian people and to urge that the parties involved engage in dialogue for the purpose of safeguarding the lives and personal safety of all the inhabitants of Panama.

8. To recommend that a new session of the Twenty-first Meeting of Consultation of Ministers of Foreign Affairs be held when appropriate to examine the Panamanian situation as a whole.

9. To instruct the Secretary General of the OAS to take the steps necessary for the implementation of this resolution.

Source: Organization of American States. Permanent Council Resolution (OEA/Ser. G CP/RES. 534 (800/89) corr. 1).

DISCUSSION QUESTIONS

1. *Given that it had not supported the Civic Crusade in past attempts to uphold the democratic process in Panama, what kind of means of intervention was the $10 million the United States gave the Civic Crusade for the 1989 elections?*

2. *Should a high-ranking official of a foreign power openly call for the violent overthrow of another government? Is this the same as calling for the assassination of a country's leader?*

3. *What obligation did the United States have to seek a multilateral solution to the crisis?*

4. *Was the Latin American view correct, that the United States was intervening in a domestic issue?*

THE UNITED STATES INVADES

After the 3 October coup, Noriega reorganized the PDF. He dispersed members of his Dignity Battalions, called "Dingbats," among units throughout the country to keep him informed about hostile plots against him. By December, Noriega had jailed and tortured more than 600 soldiers suspected of plotting against him in the October coup. While Noriega was purging the military, he called on the National Assembly to grant him additional powers. In late October, a few weeks after the failed coup attempt, the National Assembly voted unanimously to name Noriega chief of government (jefe de gobierno). As chief of government, he was commonly referred to as "Maximum Ruler." The position gave him essentially unlimited power as head of state. Noriega used the vote to demonstrate his domestic support to world leaders. He appealed to international organizations, particularly the OAS, for support against the United States. By solidifying his position in the military and the National Assembly and cracking down on civilian demonstrations, Noriega removed the mechanisms Bush had relied on for a Panamanian solution to the crisis.

As Panamanian solutions to the crisis disappeared, threats against U.S. citizens living in Panama were on the rise. U.S. soldiers were routinely stopped by Panamanian police and cited for fabricated violations. They were often fined as much as ten times the normal amount for common traffic violations, and in some cases they were jailed. Panamanian soldiers would occasionally point guns and shout obscenities at U.S. soldiers. Some U.S. troops described the tension with PDF soldiers as "a game of chicken."

The contingency plans developed by General Woerner after the May 1989 elections were increasingly considered as an option. Although the exact details of the plans are still classified, they centered around three basic proposals. The first involved a small strike by special forces units that would specifically target Noriega. The second included plans for a mid-sized attack using elements of the 193d Infantry Brigade stationed in Panama against key targets in cooperation with Panamanian units opposed to the dictator. The third involved a massive invasion designed to completely dislodge the Panamanian Defense Forces and Noriega.

The first option, a direct strike against Noriega using special forces units, was discarded. It could have been misinterpreted by the international community as a U.S. assassination plot against a foreign leader. The second option, an attack against key targets using elements of the 193d Brigade, was also ruled out due to Noriega's purging of the PDF. The purging had made it difficult to seek assistance from Panamanian military officers, and the operation was likely to produce heavy casualties for the United States without Panamanian cooperation. The third option, a massive invasion, seemed to be the most viable. The United States could cite massive opposition to Noriega and support from president elect Guillermo Endara to legitimize an invasion. A massive military strike was likely to result in less U.S. casualties because Panamanian troops would be more likely to surrender if they were overwhelmed by a large U.S. military force.

Before the United States could invade, U.S. officials needed reasons to launch the attack. Those reasons were provided during two separate events on 16 December. First, on that day Panamanian troops shot and killed a U.S. soldier. The official version of the story indicates that a group of soldiers were lost on their way to a party when they encountered a PDF roadblock near Noriega's headquarters. Fearing that the PDF troops would arrest them, they ran the roadblock, and the PDF soldiers opened fire, resulting in one American death.

Second, during a speech to the National Assembly on 16 December, Noriega claimed that the diplomatic pressure from the United States reflected a state of war against Panama. In translation from Spanish to English, however, the media in the United States reported Noriega as saying that Panama was "in a state of war" with the United States. Bush, who publicly stated that he wanted to avoid using U.S. troops in Panama, said that the PDF killing of a U.S. soldier warranted a military response. Two days later, plans for the invasion were finalized. The operation was to start at one o'clock in the morning on 20 December. It was named "Operation Just Cause."

As military officials had predicted, U.S. forces were able to suppress Panamanian troops. Most Panamanian soldiers quickly surrendered, and U.S. casualties were limited. Twenty-three U.S. soldiers died in the fighting. On 22 December, the OAS voted 20 to 1 to censure the U.S. invasion of Panama. It was the first time in its forty-two-year history that the organization had formally criticized the United States (see Table 2.2).

Noriega eluded U.S. forces for several days. Then on Christmas Eve, after Bush had placed a $1 million bounty on Noriega's head, Noriega appeared at the residence of the papal nuncio seeking asylum. Noriega had tried to reach agreements for asylum with the Cuban, Nicaraguan, and Spanish embassies. Spain refused to give the dictator refuge. U.S. soldiers had already surrounded the Cuban and Nicaraguan embassies, preventing them from giving refuge to Noriega.

On 3 January 1990, at the urging of the papal nuncio and having exhausted all other options, Noriega surrendered to U.S. authorities. Dressed in his military uniform, Noriega exited the nunciature and was taken into custody.

Noriega had been removed, but the price of the invasion had been extremely costly. Nearly a thousand Panamanians were killed. Thousands of others were left homeless. Structural damage to the country exceeded $1 billion and the economy was in shambles. Many still question whether or not Noriega's removal was legitimate and morally justified.

DISCUSSION QUESTIONS

1. *How does one decide whether the United States was militarily intervening against the state of Panama? the Noriega regime? Or, was the United States seeking to intervene on behalf of the state? the Endara government?*
2. *Were the human rights violations committed by Noriega's regime against citizens so terrible that the "fit" between the government and its people no longer existed, thereby justifying the U.S. invasion?*
3. *Were the lives of U.S. citizens and U.S. interests in Panama sufficiently threatened to warrant a military invasion?*
4. *Is the U.S. invasion of Panama more easily justified if it is interpreted as an instance of protecting the Panamanian people from a ruthless leader or as an act of self-defense on the part of the United States?*
5. *Was the use of force on the part of the United States legitimate as an expedient means of changing the government of Panama?*
6. *Was the United States ever obligated to exhaust all other avenues of peaceful resolution before initiating a military invasion?*

NOTES

1. Rear Admiral Gerald E. Gneckow, commander of U.S. Naval Forces Southern Command, in a speech to the Panamanian Chapter of the Navy League, 13 February 1990, Panama.

2. "Approximadamente 220 Civiles Panamenos Murieron en la Invasion Militar de E.U.," *El Panama America*, 11 January 1990, p. 7(A); Kevin Buckley, *Panama: The Whole Story* (N.Y.: Simon & Schuster, 1991), p. 264.

3. Zoila Rodriguez Jovane, "A Mas de Mil Millones de Balboas Ascienden Danos pos Saqueos," *La Prensa*, 21 January 1990, p. 18(A).

4. *Nunca Jamas!: Los Crimines del General Noriega (1968-1989)* (Panama: Ediciones Origines, 1990), p. 5.

5. See Buckley, *The Whole Story*, p. 20.

6. Frederick Kempe, *Divorcing the Dictator* (New York: G. P. Putnam's Sons, 1990), pp. 47-48, p. 51.

7. *Ibid.*, pp. 165-168.

8. *Ibid.*

9. Guy Gugliotta and Jeff Leen, *Kings of Cocaine* (New York: Simon and Schuster, 1989), pp. 171-173.

10. *Ibid.*, p. 175.

11. Kempe, *Divorcing the Dictator*, pp. 241-244.
12. *Ibid.*, 220-221.
13. R. M. Koster and Guillermo Sanchez, *In the Time of the Tyrants* (New York: Norton, 1990), p. 355; Kempe, *Divorcing the Dictator*, p. 253.
14. Kempe, *Divorcing the Dictator*, pp. 339-340.

FURTHER READING ON PANAMA

Books

America's Watch Report. *Human Rights in Panama*. Washington, D.C.: The America's Watch Committee, April 1988.

Buckley, Kevin. *Panama: The Whole Story*. New York: Simon and Schuster, 1991.

Dinges, John. *Our Man in Panama*. New York: Random House, 1990.

Kempe, Frederick. *Divorcing the Dictator: America's Bungled Affair with Noriega*. New York: G. P. Putnam's Sons, 1990.

Marques, Jaime G. *Panama en la Encrucijada: Colonia o Nacion?* Panama: Impreso en Editora Renovacion Comercial, 1989.

Mellander, G. A. *The United States in Panamanian Politics: The Intriguing Formative Years*. Danville, Ill.: Interstate Printers and Publishers, 1971.

National Banking Commission of Panama. "Reporte Balance de Situacion," 24 January 1990. Mimeograph.

Organization of American States Inter-American Commission on Human Rights. Report on the Situation of Human Rights in Panama. Washington, D.C.: The Organization of American States, 1989.

Priestly, George. *Military Government and Popular Participation in Panama*. Boulder and London: Westview Press, 1986.

The Puebla Institute. *Panama Without Law: A Compilation of Human Rights Statements*. Washington, D.C.: The Puebla Institute, 1989.

Articles

Chase, James, "Getting to Sack the General," *New York Review of Books* 35, no. 7 (28 April 1988): 49-55.

Massing, Michael, "What Ever Happened to Panama?" *New York Review of Books* 37, no. 8 (17 May 1990): 43-49.

Millet, Richard, "The Aftermath of Intervention: Panama 1990," *Journal of Interamerican Studies* 32, no. 1 (Spring 1990): 1-16.

Sullivan, Mark P., "Panama's Political Crisis: Prospects and U.S. Policy Concerns," *Report from the U.S. Foreign Affairs and National Defense Division*, Washington, D.C. Updated 2 March 1989.

3

A FRAGILE AGREEMENT: THE 1972 VIETNAMESE PEACE NEGOTIATIONS

This case study shares an obvious similarity with the Panama case. It shows U.S. officials taking measures to end a long-term relationship with an ally; a relationship that is both domestically unpopular and increasingly detrimental to U.S. interests abroad. Like the Panama case, this case raises questions about the morality of means.

U.S. officials engaged in secrecy and concealment in the 1972 diplomatic efforts in order to extricate the United States from the Vietnam War. In entering the secret negotiations, the United States was seeking what President Richard Nixon termed "peace with honor"—a military, not a political, resolution to the war. The South Vietnamese government, headed by Nguyen Van Thieu, did not want a negotiated settlement with the North Vietnamese and feared that its powerful ally, the United States, would seek a settlement that left South Vietnam politically and militarily vulnerable to the North. The United States recognized the legitimacy of South Vietnam as a sovereign state, yet it felt that any chance of success required excluding South Vietnam from the bargaining table.

This chapter is an edited version of the case study by Allan E. Goodman, The Vietnam Negotiations, October-December 1972, *Pew case study no. 307.*

The exclusion of South Vietnamese representatives from the secret negotiations with Hanoi raises ethical questions about the nature and necessity of secrecy and concealment in international negotiations. Does secrecy have a place in international negotiations? Does secrecy create a negotiating environment in which there is a greater chance of success? During the negotiations, Henry Kissinger briefed Thieu in general terms only and did not inform him of the details of the agreement until both Hanoi and Washington had tentatively approved the draft. What did the United States owe South Vietnam in terms of loyalty and fair representation at the negotiating table in Paris? Was the exclusion of South Vietnam from the negotiations a prerequisite for success? And if so, whose success and at whose expense?

*   *   *

The story behind the breakthrough on 8 October 1972, in the secret negotiations between Washington and Hanoi, and especially the breakdown in those negotiations on 22 October, begins in mid-summer of that year. By July, U.S. government officials had three indications that Hanoi might be prepared to negotiate an end to the war.

First, Hanoi's tone in the secret meetings between Henry Kissinger and Le Duc Tho changed from hostility to cordiality. Second, U.S. officials concluded from intelligence reports and captured Communist documents that Hanoi had begun to instruct its cadres in South Vietnam to prepare to compete politically with the Thieu government. Third, prisoner of war interrogation reports, moreover, indicated that the communists' military leadership had planned a series of land-grabbing operations in the early fall to extend their apparent area of control in anticipation of a cease-fire-in-place. Consequently, Kissinger visited Saigon in late July to brief South Vietnamese President Nguyen Van Thieu on the secret talks. This was done partly to reassure Thieu that current press speculation predicting breakthroughs, which would involve either his ouster or U.S. support for a coalition government, was groundless. Technically, of course, this was correct. But Kissinger did not indicate to Thieu that, due to the indications mentioned above, he personally expected to reach an agreement with Hanoi.

In taking this step to brief Thieu, but only in general terms, Kissinger probably believed that trying to win Thieu's support before Hanoi was committed to a specific agreement would imperil the whole negotiating process. Kissinger feared that Thieu would leak details of the expected agreement, rally public opinion against it, and denounce Hanoi. He thought Thieu would be easier to persuade if he were presented with a fait accompli and then either given extensive military supplies before the agreement went into effect or if the North Vietnamese Army (NVA) were dealt a military setback that be assured that there would be no offensive during the 1973 dry season.

Kissinger doubted that Thieu would support the agreement without the above conditions, even if the agreement were underpinned by understandings with Moscow and Peking that Hanoi would not be resupplied with the means to continue to wage conventional, large-unit warfare.

Kissinger and Tho met twice in August. For the first time in ten years of secret talks, the North Vietnamese negotiators were talking about a South Vietnam where a communist and a non-communist army and administration would have to coexist, and Kissinger interpreted this rhetoric as a sign that Hanoi would not insist on Thieu's ouster. Shortly after the second meeting ended, Tho returned to Hanoi for consultations. Kissinger believed that the politburo would soon make a decision between war and peace. He again went to Saigon to meet with Thieu.

Unfortunately, Thieu believed Kissinger was wrong about Hanoi's willingness to negotiate a settlement of war. In a speech to the National Defense College in Saigon in August 1972, Thieu set out what he thought was ahead:

> There is only one way to force the Communists to negotiate seriously, and that consists of the total destruction of their economic and war potential. We must strike at them continuously, relentlessly, denying them any moment to catch their breath. . . . If our allies are determined, peace will be restored in Indochina. If they lack determination, the Communists will revert to their half-guerilla-half-conventional warfare, and the war will go on in Indochina forever.[1]

By 1972, the gap between Washington's and Saigon's expectations with respect to when, and on what terms, a negotiated settlement could be achieved was very wide. Kissinger sensed this during his discussions with Thieu, but he failed to adequately consider the possibility that, when an agreement had been reached, Thieu would refuse to sign, or that President Nixon would permit Thieu to block a chance to have a negotiated settlement before the November election.

Another indication that Hanoi was ready to reach a negotiated settlement came on 11 September. On that day, the communist Provisional Revolutionary Government of South Vietnam (hereafter referred to as the PRG) released what it described as an "important statement on ending . . . the war . . . and restoration of peace." The essence of that statement was the following proposal.

> If a correct solution is to be found to the Viet Nam problem, and a lasting peace ensured in Viet Nam, the U.S. government must meet the two following requirements:

1. To respect the Vietnamese people's right to true independence and the South Vietnamese people's right to effective self-determination: stop the U.S. war of aggression in Viet Nam; stop the bombing, mining, and blockade of the democratic republic of Viet Nam; completely cease the Vietnamization policy; terminate all U.S. military activities in South Viet Nam; rapidly and completely withdraw from South Viet Nam all U.S. troops, advisors, military personnel, technical personnel, weapons, and war materials and those of the other foreign countries in the U.S. camp; liquidate the U.S. military bases in South Viet Nam; stop supporting the Nguyen Van Thieu stooge administration.

2. A solution to the internal problem of South Viet Nam must stem from the actual situation: there exist in South Viet Nam two administrations, two armies, and other political forces. It is necessary to achieve national concord: the parties of South Viet Nam must unite on the basis of equality, mutual respect, and mutual nonelimination; democratic freedoms must be guaranteed to the people. To this end, it is necessary to form in South Viet Nam a provisional government of national concord with three equal segments to take charge of the affairs of the period of transition and to organize truly free and democratic general elections.[2]

Kissinger detected in the PRG's proposal a willingness to settle for a cease-fire first, leaving the solution of internal political problems to subsequent negotiations between the South Vietnamese government (hereafter referred to as "Saigon" or GVN) and the PRG. He also queried Soviet leader Leonid Brezhnev, himself fresh from talks with Le Duc Tho, and was assured that the PRG announcement signaled the beginning of real negotiations.

When Kissinger and Tho met on 15 September, Kissinger, therefore made a personal plea for progress in the negotiations. As it stood, Kissinger said, the PRG proposal was not acceptable to President Nixon because it still implied that the United States and not the South Vietnamese people would remove Thieu from office. If the North Vietnamese could be more flexible on that point, Kissinger urged, they would find a president more eager to reach a negotiated settlement than he was at that moment. But, he warned, after the election the president's position might very well harden, the prospects for negotiations dim, and the war continue.

At the next secret meeting (26 September 1972) Le Duc Tho proposed creating a tripartite National Council of Reconciliation and Concord (NCRC) that, while composed of the three equal segments, was not to be considered a government (something the PRG wanted) and that would make decisions only on the principle of unanimity. Kissinger realized that this would be acceptable to President Nixon and thought it should be far more acceptable to Thieu than prior proposals which called for Thieu's resignation.[3]

Kissinger and Tho met again on 8 October. The meeting, however, began with few signs that it would lead anywhere. To the American participants in the meeting, Tho seemed suddenly truculent in tone and flatly stated that it was impossible to separate the military from a political settlement and demanded the resignation of Thieu as president of South Vietnam. However, just before the meeting was scheduled to conclude, Tho asked for a brief recess. When he returned, Tho handed Kissinger an English-language version of a draft agreement. Initially, it appeared to Kissinger as though Hanoi's draft could be the basis for at least an end to the fighting in South Vietnam, if not a political settlement of the war. The draft proposed an immediate cease-fire, U.S troop withdrawal, and prisoner of war exchange. Each of these developments were to proceed according to a timetable which appeared independent of any progress made toward a political settlement. As Le Duc Tho described these and other features of the agreement in Vietnamese, however, U.S. language experts quickly realized that the terms used to describe the draft agreement in Vietnamese were ambiguous or objectionable and would certainly be opposed by the South Vietnamese government.

Kissinger viewed the draft as a significant breakthrough. As he later told the press, the North Vietnamese government:

> dropped their demand for a coalition government which would absorb all existing authority. They dropped their demand for a veto over the personalities and the structure of the existing government. They agreed for the first time to a formula which permitted a simultaneous discussion of Laos and Cambodia. In short, we had for the first time a framework where, rather than exchange general propositions and measure our progress by whether dependent clauses of particular sentences had been minutely altered, we could examine concretely and precisely where we stood and what each side was prepared to give.[4]

Of particular concern to Kissinger's staff, in contrast, was a passage in the draft which called for the creation of an administrative structure to achieve national reconciliation and concord, called in English the National Council on Reconciliation and Concord (NCRC). In Vietnamese the phrase "administrative structure" implied that such a body would have actual governmental authority. Thieu was certain to reject this portion of the draft.

Kissinger and Tho recessed their negotiations on 12 October so that Kissinger could take the draft to Washington. There, he vetted it, decided to pursue further negotiations, and returned to Paris on 17 October to tighten up the language and organize the agreement into a final, acceptable form. Le Duc Tho indicated that Hanoi wanted the agreement signed by the end of

October, and Kissinger promised he would do his utmost to meet this apparent deadline.

DISCUSSION QUESTIONS

1. *What were the reasons for Kissinger's decision to brief Thieu and his govern-ment in general terms only about the U.S secret negotiations with Hanoi? Are they morally justified reasons?*
2. *Did the United States have an obligation to help the South and North find an equitable solution to the domestic problem of self-governance?*
3. *What responsibilities, morally speaking, did the United States have to the South Vietnamese government? To the South Vietnamese people?*
4. *Did South Vietnam have a right to remain politically independent from the North?*

LAYING OUT THE DETAILS TO THIEU

Throughout this period, Thieu and his ambassador in Paris had been briefed in only the most general terms about the details of the secret talks. Thieu had not been informed of the breakthrough in early October, nor of the fact that an actual text had been prepared. Kissinger left Paris for Saigon on 17 October, confident that he could persuade Thieu to accept the agreement and that it could be initialed by 22 October, as Hanoi insisted.

Arriving in Saigon, Kissinger briefed U.S. Ambassador Ellsworth Bunker, General Creighton Abrams (the commander of U.S. forces in Vietnam), and Bunker's deputy, Ambassador Charles Whitehouse. Bunker and Creighton were optimistic, based on what they had heard, that an agreement could be reached. They assessed the situation as one in which the United States was either going to have to fight for another year or withdraw its troops. Neither option would bring any gains. In addition, the North Vietnamese had launched a "high point" offensive in order to seize as much territory as possible before a cease-fire was agreed to.

Charles Whitehouse agreed with Bunker and Creighton that an agreement would be possible. But Whitehouse cautioned that the time frame was too short. As Kissinger remembered the conversation:

For Saigon to cut the umbilical cord with the United States would be a wrenching psychological blow. Thieu would need many weeks to prepare himself and his people for it. No matter what the terms, Thieu would prevaricate and delay as long as possible.[5]

Kissinger presented Thieu with an English draft of the agreement and spent three-and-one-half-hours explaining its importance on 19 October 1972. Kissinger wanted the South Vietnamese president to understand not only that the agreement made sense and protected Saigon's interests, but also that it would be difficult for the United States government to resist signing it. In his first meeting with Thieu, Kissinger explained that the Nixon administration was being pressured by significant domestic support for an end to the war.

Thieu's response was noncommittal and cryptic. Aside from showing Kissinger and his delegation at the outset of their first meeting very little deference or courtesy, Thieu appeared merely to question some of the details of the draft, not Kissinger's interpretation and defense of it. Additional meetings with Thieu and his advisors were then scheduled. The next day, however, the Kissinger-Thieu discussions took a turn for the worse. Thieu and his advisors revealed that they did not agree with Kissinger's interpretation of the language of the agreement.

Linguistic problems and ambiguities indicated deeper and fundamental problems for Thieu's advisors. They had read between the lines of each provision in the draft to find evidence of Hanoi's perfidy, just as, it will be recalled, Kissinger's staff had done when they first read the Vietnamese version of the draft Le Duc Tho had prepared on 8 October. For example, in the provisions concerning troop withdrawal, the term for U.S. soldiers was actually slang meaning "dirty yankee soldier." Within a day, Thieu's advisors had discovered some 129 linguistic changes that were "essential" before the documents could be signed by the GVN.

Saigon also had fundamental objections to the principle of cease-fire-in-place on which the agreement rested. Although Thieu had long suspected that Washington was willing to settle for such a cease-fire, he was no more inclined to accept it in 1972 than he had been in 1969, when his suspicion had first been aroused. Thieu saw the agreement as virtually guaranteeing that there would be continued warfare over the location of the front lines. Finally, Thieu argued that the provisions concerning inspection were weak. Of greatest concern was the absence of any reference to the status of the demilitarized zone (DMZ) and of any provision for an alternate means of obtaining a political settlement, should the two parties fail to reach an agreement within the prescribed ninety day period for their negotiations.

In response, Kissinger questioned why Saigon was afraid, since the GVN had the advantage of a million-man army that was well-trained and well-equipped. Thieu's reply was that South Vietnam was a nation of only eighteen million people, and the costly maintenance of a large defense force would reduce the supply of potential development resources, resulting in his government's perpetual dependence on U.S. aid. Thieu also was deeply suspicious of the administrative structure to be set by the NCRC, and labeled it a disguised coalition.

For the remainder of his visit, Kissinger tried a step-by-step approach in the negotiations with Thieu. He responded to each of the South Vietnamese objections to the agreement individually, and made considerable progress in reducing the changes Saigon desired, from a list of more than one hundred down to a more manageable number of twenty-six. On the morning of 21 October, Kissinger met with the Foreign Minister of South Vietnam and his experts to go over the agreement and their proposed changes draft revisions. Over lunch with Ambassador Ellsworth Bunker, Kissinger described his and Bunker's outlooks as "quite optimistic" as they awaited details on their next meeting with Thieu. Both expected such a meeting would occur that afternoon. Ominously, there was no call from Thieu's aides to arrange such a meeting. Later that evening Kissinger and Bunker were informed that Thieu would see them the next morning at 8 a.m. Thieu also called Ambassador Bunker and emotionally accused the U.S. of attempting to plot a coup to overthrow him. Kissinger considered the call as a bad omen for the meeting ahead and indicative of the frenzied, hostile atmosphere within Thieu's circle of advisors. But as Kissinger observed:

The meeting with Thieu at 8:00 a.m. the next morning, Sunday, October 22, did not, after the ominous preliminaries, produce a confrontation. Indeed, it almost seemed as if Thieu had staged the melodrama of the previous day to establish a posture of independence that would make it possible for him to go along with us at the last moment. Thieu restated his by now familiar objections to the agreement. He focused on the continued presence of North Vietnamese troops and on the composition of the National Council, which had no functions, in which he was to have a veto, and which, as it turned out, never came into being. I answered Thieu's concerns point by point . . . Thieu responded with some dignity that for us the problem was how to end our participation in the war; for him it was a matter of life and death for his country. He had to consider not only the terms of the agreement but the perception of it by the people of South Vietnam. He was therefore consulting with the leaders of the National Assembly. He also wanted to hear a full report from his advisers on our reaction to the charges they proposed. He would meet Bunker and me again at 5:00 p.m. . . . to give us his final reply. Bunker and I left the meeting encouraged. "I think we finally made a breakthrough," I optimistically cabled Washington.[6]

When this meeting was held, Thieu's reluctance to adhere to the provisions of the proposal was apparent. He justified his skepticism of communist intentions by referring to an interview that had been held between North Vietnam's premier Pham Van Dong and *Newsweek*'s senior editor Arnaud de

Borchgrave on 18 October. Pham Van Dong began the interview with references to the failure of Vietnamization and the great victory that the North Vietnamese government's (hereafter referred to as "Hanoi" or DRVN) 1972 Easter military offensive symbolized; he described the United States from that point on as being forced to liquidate its commitments to Saigon. When asked if South Vietnamese president Thieu could participate in the process of political settlement that would follow the war, Pham replied: "Thieu has been overtaken by events." De Borchgrave asked what would happen after a cease-fire. Pham replied: "The situation will then be two armies and two administrations in the south, and given that situation, they will have to work out their own arrangements for a . . . coalition of transition."[7]

When the meeting with Thieu ended, Kissinger had to cable Washington that Thieu "rejected the entire plan or any modification of it and refuses to discuss any further negotiations on the basis of it."[8]

DISCUSSION QUESTIONS

1. *Given the significance of the breakthrough in negotiations in early October, was Thieu entitled to know as soon as possible what the details of the proposed cease-fire were and the fact that a written draft existed?*
2. *Given the degree of domestic pressure on the Nixon administration to end U.S. involvement in the war, was Kissinger obligated to pursue the interests of the United States at the cost of South Vietnamese independence?*
3. *Did the proposed cease-fire-in-place fulfill U.S. obligations to the Thieu government?*
4. *Because South Vietnam could not fight without the economic and military assistance of the United States, did it have a right to self-determination?*
5. *Did the South Vietnamese people earn the right to their "nationhood" by the degree of violence they were willing to use to retain their political independence from the North?*

FROM BREAKTHROUGH TO BREAKDOWN

On 24 October, South Vietnamese President Thieu publicly denounced the agreement as a ruse designed to provide the NVA with time to regroup its forces and to provide the communists with a clear opportunity to gain political control of South Vietnam. Thieu believed they would do this by joining forces with his opponents, pressing with them for his ouster, and then subverting the police and army which would leave the country extremely vulnerable to a new North Vietnamese military offensive. To avoid being placed in such a position, Thieu renewed his demand for the withdrawal of all NVA forces from South Vietnam and declared in a national radio address that in order to be prepared for a cease-fire "the communist infrastructure must be wiped out quickly and mercilessly."[9]

Hanoi responded to Thieu's statements in a radio broadcast of its own the next day which excoriated him personally, blasted the Nixon administration for sabotaging a chance to end the war, and demanded that the Kissinger-Tho agreement be signed by 31 October. To Hanoi, concluding an agreement within a few days was essential. In the rush to claim insecure territory to enlarge the area of communist control with a cease-fire-in-place, many PRG military units revealed themselves prematurely and were now the targets of GVN police and army attacks. The North Vietnamese also feared that Washington would try to strengthen Saigon's war-fighting capability significantly if protracted negotiations ensued.

At this point, and also resorting to public diplomacy, Kissinger called a press conference for 26 October (his first on national television) the purpose of which "was to rescue from Vietnamese hatreds a fragile agreement that would end a decade of agony." The press conference was designed to "reassure Hanoi that we would stand by the basic agreement," leave open "the possibility of raising Saigon's suggested changes," and "convey to Saigon that we were determined to proceed on course."[10] Kissinger expected that further negotiations with both Hanoi and Saigon would be required to complete the agreement. But as he told the press: "What stands in the way of an agreement now are issues that are relatively less important than those that have already been settled." It was in this context that Kissinger made his ill-fated statement that "Peace is at hand."

But Hanoi did not respond to Washington's requests to resume negotiations until 4 November. The date the North Vietnamese proposed was 14 November. On 7 November, Kissinger replied by proposing 15 November (to enable his assistant, General Alexander Haig, to travel to Saigon in an effort this time to assure Thieu's concurrence with the U.S. negotiating approach). Hanoi replied to this proposal on 8 November and postponed the date further, suggesting 20 November and indicating that Le Duc Tho was currently ill. On 9 November the U.S. agreed to a meeting on the 20th.

When the Kissinger-Tho negotiations resumed in Paris, they did so in an atmosphere of hostility and mistrust, resulting, according to Kissinger, in a series of "sterile exchanges" over the specific issues[11] (see Table 3.1). Le Duc Tho appeared wary of Kissinger and his authority, apparently thinking Kissinger had negotiated an agreement in October that exceeded his instructions and failed to persuade Nixon and Thieu to accept it. The U.S. side was increasingly alarmed, moreover, about apparent communist plans to use the first few days and weeks of post-agreement confusion as a screen for attacks against the GVN. And from the start, Kissinger was particularly

TABLE 3.1 Central Issues in the Vietnam Negotiations November-December 1972

Central Issues	DRVN/PRG Position	U.S./GVN Position
Civilian Political Prisoners	Release of civilian political prisoners should be linked to releasing POWs	Release of civilian political prisoners independent of U.S. POWs
American Civilian Technicians	Technicians should be withdrawn along with U.S. troops	Technicians should be allowed to stay
National Council of Reconciliation and Concord	Should be called an "administrative structure" in the agreement and imply actual government authority	Should simply be called the NCRC and imply no such authority
Status of the Demilitarized Zone	Legal status of DMZ to be discussed after agreement signed	Both sides should be obligated to respect DMZ as demarcation line between North and South Vietnam; military movement across it prohibited
NVA in the South	The NVA should be allowed to remain as part of a cease-fire in place	The new units that came south to participate in the Easter Offensive should be withdrawn; other NVA units can remain
Cease-fire in Laos	To follow 30 days after an agreement	Should allow an agreement within a week to 10 days
Machinery of the International Commission on Control and Supervision (ICCS)	Can only investigate a report with unanimous approval of members; no independent logistical capability	Should be strengthened and in place at the time agreement goes into effect
Resupply of weapons to the GVN	Only "worn out or damaged" weapons could be replaced	"Destroyed" or "used up" weapons could be replaced
Signing Procedures	All parties should sign agreement and be named in it	Two virtually identical agreements to be signed: one between the U.S. and the DRVN on behalf of the GVN and PRG and another that referred only to "the parties participating in the Paris Conference," which U.S. and GVN would sign on one page and the DRVN and PRG on another

Source: Allan E. Goodman, *The Lost Peace: America's Search for a Negotiated Settlement of the Vietnam War* (Stanford, Calif.: Hoover Institution Press, 1978), pp. 186-187.

worried about his lack of leverage on Hanoi in the face of a likely congressional cutoff of further funds for the war.

In the meetings which followed with Hanoi, Kissinger represented both Washington and Saigon. He put forward some 69 linguistic and other changes in the agreement demanded by President Thieu but largely "to avoid the charge that we were less than meticulous in guarding Saigon's concerns" since Thieu had been warned "there was no possibility of obtaining this many changes." In retrospect, Kissinger considers the putting forward of all of Thieu's demands "a major tactical mistake" because "it must have strengthened Hanoi's already strong temptation to dig in its heels and push me against our Congressional deadlines."[12]

The other set of issues Kissinger introduced represented the minimum demands of the United States: unless they were satisfied, Kissinger told Tho, an agreement could not be signed. These demands centered on the problems likely to occur in the first few weeks and months that the agreement was in force, problems raised by expected military operations aimed at extending communist territorial control. It was essential to Kissinger, for example, that the cease-fire supervisory mechanism be in place and able to function effectively when the agreement was signed. Equally essential was the clarification of the military status of the DMZ, an issue that Thieu wanted raised because it directly affected the sovereignty of the GVN. Kissinger's approach was to downplay the sovereignty aspect of this issue and to discuss the DMZ in terms of its role in assuring that there would be a cease-fire. Consistent with its objective of retaining an unimpaired capability to resume the military struggle if the political evolution specified in the agreement did not occur, Hanoi had sought only the vaguest of characterizations of the DMZ.

Kissinger's strategy for dealing with all of the linguistic problems posed by the agreement's translation into Vietnamese was to delete as many of the ambiguous or objectionable phrases as possible. Issues of principle that could not be included in the actual text of the agreement because Hanoi flatly refused to commit itself publicly to them were left to a series of understandings that became part of the official, classified record.

The basic tightening up of the agreement sought by Washington did not come easily. As Kissinger was methodically working through the U.S. agenda, the North Vietnamese were introducing new demands as the implied price for making the changes Washington sought. In the November meetings, for example, Hanoi reintroduced demands for the removal of Thieu as South Vietnam's president, the simultaneous release of political prisoners with the POW's and a significant strengthening rather than diminution of the powers of the National Council of Reconciliation and Concord, the body in which the communist PRG would have equal voice with the GVN over future political evolution in South Vietnam. Frequently, also, Hanoi would negotiate by dropping its insistence on the wording of a particular article of the agreement, only to have the objectionable wording, appear in its version of "understandings" referred to above.

One of the U.S. negotiators recalled that

there was clearly an attitude of dalliance on Hanoi's part, and it was then that Nixon told us to begin warning Hanoi in no uncertain terms that a failure to negotiate seriously would result in a renewal of the bombing. Serious negotiations from our perspective meant that Hanoi should cooperate in clarifying the linguistic ambiguities, working out the protocols, and staying within the framework of the October draft."[13]

Such warnings and expectations were conveyed to Le Duc Tho in a ninety minute meeting on 24 November. At that meeting, Kissinger also pointedly warned Hanoi thereafter that the bombing, suspended in October, based on the president's prediction that an agreement was near, could be easily resumed, with a much greater intensity.

DISCUSSION QUESTIONS

1. *What options, politically speaking, did Thieu have instead of going public with his disagreement with Kissinger over the tentative agreement?*
2. *The cut off of congressional funds for the war would have further weakened Kissinger's negotiating position with Hanoi. Could he have politically and morally abandoned Thieu at this point and gone for a settlement favorable to U.S. interests?*
3. *A conflict of ends existed between the United States and South Vietnam. But to what extent were Thieu's interests also U.S. interests?*

CLOSING OFF OPTIONS

The next round of the negotiations lasted from 4-14 December. From the start of this round, it was clear to Kissinger that Hanoi, in the person of Le Duc Tho, was unwilling to do more than posture and accuse the U.S. government of bad faith. Nevertheless, Kissinger still hoped that all remaining issues could be settled by diplomacy and proposed to Tho a specific scenario that would lead to signing and agreement before Christmas.

However, as Kissinger reported to President Nixon in a cable after the first day of meetings, Le Duc Tho

rejected every change we asked for, asked for a change on civilian prisoners requiring all those alleged to be held by Saigon to be released simultaneously with the release of military POW's, demanded the withdrawal of American civilians from South Vietnam thus making the maintenance of the Vietnam air force impossible, and withdrew some concessions from last week. In short, we would wind up with an agreement significantly worse than what we started with. I told him flatly that his approach did not provide the basis for a settlement. In the ensuing dialogue Tho stuck firmly by his intransigent position. The only alternative he offered to his presentation this afternoon was to go back to the October agreement literally with no changes by either side.[14]

Late in the evening of 5 December and after Kissinger and his staff had "spent hours . . . seeking to distill some ray of hope" from what Le Duc Tho had said, Kissinger concluded "that the only hope of averting a collapse would be messages to Moscow and Peking."[15]   These messages contained Kissinger's appraisal that the resumed talks were leading nowhere, that a "breakup" was "probable," and that the U.S. would have to react militarily to avert or break a deadlock. The Chinese never responded to Kissinger's message. Moscow "counseled patience, expressed confidence in Hanoi's desire for peace, and assured us . . . that the North Vietnamese were still ready to sign an agreement within the October framework."[16] Nevertheless, when the talks resumed on 6 and 7 December, Kissinger found only "continued procrastination" on the part of Hanoi.[17] There also ensued a series of telegraphic exchanges between Nixon and Kissinger which convinced the president that there was "no way of sustaining an effective negotiation strategy" through the administration's public diplomacy. "Only fear of resumed military operations would keep Hanoi on course.[18]

Kissinger and Tho met again on 6 December. Both sides reviewed their positions and emended individual clauses. Le Duc Tho continued to refuse to allow experts from both sides to meet and negotiate the detailed protocols even on provisions not in dispute. Le Duc Tho informed Kissinger that they were "studying our documents" and theirs were not prepared. In effect, Tho was stalling. Another meeting was held the next day, at which point Kissinger concluded that to Hanoi, "the lapse of time could only improve its position." Thus, to Kissinger "December 7 marked the beginning of the real deadlock."[19]

Over the next seven days, Hanoi managed to keep an agreement in view but effectively out of reach. On 8 December, Tho allowed what Kissinger termed "major steps forward" with respect to the authority of the NCRC (it was no longer to be called even an "administrative" structure because that phrase still translated into Vietnamese in a way that suggested the Council would have actual government authority) and the separation of the issue of freeing civilian and military POW's, but made unacceptable demands with respect to the status of the DMZ and essentially prohibited American technicians from helping South Vietnam to maintain its air force. This latter issue was conceded by Tho the next day but he insisted that military movement through the DMZ be permitted. When Kissinger proposed a compromise that would permit civilians and non-military officials to move across the DMZ, Tho, apparently taken aback, "suddenly complained of a headache, high blood pressure, general debility"[20] which required what amounted to a 48 hour recess until 11 December.

When Kissinger and Tho met again, Tho scuttled other parts of the agreement and said that his instructions on the status of the DMZ would not arrive until the next day.

On 12 December, Tho indicated that he had at last received instructions from Hanoi on the status of the DMZ.

He had a proposal that omitted the phrase "civilian" from any formula for permitted movement across the DMZ. In other words, Hanoi wanted to leave open the right of military transit through a Demilitarized Zone, one of the neater tricks of diplomacy, and one that raised even further doubts about the ban on infiltration. To ease our pain, Tho finally produced protocols for the cease-fire and international control machinery. He now preempted our plans by informing me that he had decided to leave Paris for Hanoi on Thursday, December 14, taking four or five days to get there. He would not be able to settle unless he could personally convert the recalcitrants in the Politburo who were constantly giving him a hard time, especially on the DMZ. He offered to return if necessary, but thought we could settle the remaining issues by an exchange of messages, a patent absurdity given the many technical details still requiring attention. The idea of a pacific Tho constrained by his bellicose peers from making concessions was mind-boggling; but it served Tho's purpose of stalling without (he hoped) giving an excuse to retaliate.[21]

At this point, Kissinger cabled Nixon that he had concluded from the last meeting that Hanoi was stringing the United States along. Their consistent pattern is to give us just enough each day "to keep us going but nothing decisive which could conclude an agreement."[22] Kissinger also pointed out that by doing this, Hanoi was being careful in not giving the United States a pretext for resuming bombing.

Kissinger believed that each day of his latest round of negotiations brought the United States and Hanoi "further away from an agreement."[23] The more Hanoi stalled, the less likely a negotiated settlement would be reached.

In his final cable from Paris, Kissinger argued that the United States had "two essential strategic choices." First, to play hard ball with Hanoi and resume bombing and other means of violent coercion. "This would include measures like reseeding the mines, massive two-day strikes against the power plants over this weekend, and a couple of B-52 efforts. This would make clear that they paid something for these past ten days." In addition, Kissinger argued for pressures to be placed on Thieu so that both sides knew the United States would no longer tolerate intransigence.

Second, the United States could continue to play Tho's game and schedule another meeting in early January. This course of action would "test the extremely unlikely hypothesis that Tho might get new instructions." By appearing cooperative and allowing Hanoi time, the United States, if stonewalled again by Hanoi, could then justify resuming the bombing and blame both Vietnamese parties but place the major responsibility on Hanoi. At that point, the United States "would offer a bilateral deal of withdrawal and an end of bombing for prisoners."[24]

Back in Washington, and deeply pessimistic about prospects for further productive negotiations, Kissinger and Nixon feared that Hanoi was now going to revert to the tactics of stalling for time in the expectation that U.S. domestic pressures and the rift between Washington and Saigon would force acceptance of an agreement that gave communist Provisional Revolutionary Government (PRG) actual political authority and that allowed the North Vietnamese Army to operate with impunity in South Vietnam. Thus, as Kissinger writes in his memoirs, when

> Nixon, Haig and I met on the morning of December 14 to consider our course . . . we were agreed that if we did nothing we would wind up paralyzed. . . . There was no reason to expect Hanoi to change its tactics if talks did resume in January . . . we had only two choices: Taking a massive, shocking step to impose our will on events and end the war quickly, or letting matters drift into another round of inconclusive negotiations, prolonged warfare, bitter national divisions, and mounting casualties. There were no other options.[25]

The bombing of Hanoi and Haiphong for eleven consecutive days began on 18 December.

DISCUSSION QUESTIONS

1. *At what cost (morally and politically) was Kissinger willing to salvage the agreement?*
2. *Was the Nixon administration simply willing to get its hands dirty by opting for the bombing of the cities of Hanoi and Haiphong?*
3. *What responsibility did Kissinger have for exhausting all avenues to a peaceful resolution? Had he met them?*

4. *Was the decision to bomb North Vietnam the most responsible action the United States could have taken given the circumstances?*

NOTES

1. Translated in Allan E. Goodman's *The Lost Peace: America's Search for A Negotiated Peace Settlement of the Vietnam War.* (Stanford, Calif.: Hoover Institution Press, 1978), p. 126.

2. *Ibid.*, p. 127.

3. Prophetically, however, only three days later in a speech to Saigon University students, Thieu declared: "If the United States accepts to withdraw its troops unconditionally [without insisting that Hanoi do the same], the Communists will win militarily. If we accept a coalition, we will lose politically." *Ibid.*, p. 129. Throughout the summer and fall of 1973 Thieu never wavered in his conviction that, despite whatever the North Vietnamese called the organization to be created as part of a political settlement, it was a disguised coalition.

4. Henry Kissinger, press conference, 26 October 1972.

5. Henry Kissinger, *White House Years* (Boston: Little, Brown and Co., 1979), p. 1367.

6. *Ibid.*, p. 1382.

7. "Exclusive from Hanoi", *Newsweek*, 30 October 1972, p. 26.

8. *Ibid.*, p. 1385.

9. Goodman, *The Lost Peace*, p. 138.

10. Kissinger, *White House Years*, p. 1398.

11. *Ibid.*, p. 1427.

12. *Ibid.*

13. Goodman, *The Lost Peace*, p. 158.

14. Kissinger, *White House Years*, p. 1429.

15. *Ibid.*, pp. 1429-1430.

16. *Ibid.*, p. 1432.

17. *Ibid.*, p. 1434.

18. *Ibid.*, p. 1431.

19. *Ibid.*, p. 1434.

20. *Ibid.*, p. 1437.

21. *Ibid.*, p. 1441.

22. *Ibid.*, p. 1442.

23. *Ibid.*, p. 1444.

24. *Ibid.*, pp. 1444-1445.

25. *Ibid.*, pp. 1447-1448.

FURTHER READING ON THE VIETNAMESE NEGOTIATIONS

Books

Duncanson, Dennis J. *Government and Revolution in Vietnam.* Oxford: Oxford University Press, 1968.

Herz, Martin F. *The Vietnam War in Retrospect.* Washington, D.C.: School of Foreign Service, Georgetown University, 1968.

Karnow, Stanley. *Vietnam: A History.* New York: Penguin Books, 1984.

Kolko, Gabriel. *Anatomy of a War: Vietnam, the United States and the Modern Historical Experience.* New York: Pantheon Books, 1985.

Nixon, Richard M. *No More Vietnams.* New York: Arbor House, 1985.

Turley, William S. *The Second Indochina War.* Boulder, Colo.: Westview Press, 1986.

4

SHARING A GLOBAL COMMONS: THE THIRD UNITED NATIONS CONFERENCE ON THE LAW OF THE SEA

This case study focuses on the Third United Nations Conference on the Law of the Sea (UNCLOS III), which was an attempt to obtain international consensus on issues regarding ownership and rights of usage of ocean resources. Herein we examine the ends that drive distributive patterns and raise questions about the morality of those ends and the justness of the distribution.

As part of UNCLOS III, it was proposed that ocean resources be recognized as the "common heritage of mankind" to be shared in an equitable manner among nations. The United States and other countries with the technology to mine the mineral-rich nodules of the deep seabed argued that those resources belonged to no one. The marketplace would determine who could economically benefit from the mining of the nodules. Developing countries, lacking the technology, sought to establish an international regime

This chapter is an edited version of the case study by Steven R. David and Peter Digeser, The United States and the Law of the Sea Treaty, *Pew case study no. 418.*

that would control the mining and divide the revenues equitably among nations. Do ocean resources belong to everyone, as the phrase "common heritage of mankind" implies? Or do the resources belong to no one, available for exploitation by anyone who has the technology to do so?

Extensive divisions also emerged on issues regarding freedom of the seas, offshore oil drilling, and fishing. Archipelagic states wanted "archipelagic waters" plus a 200-mile economic zone. Latin American countries, fearing the encroachment of U.S. navy ships, oil tankers, and fishing fleets, advocated extending their sovereignty to a 200-mile economic zone. By contrast, the maritime powers, the United States, the United Kingdom, and the Soviet Union, pressed for narrower territorial waters and "unimpeded transit" through straits for military and strategic economic purposes. Eventually, conflicting national ends and distrust of any international authority on the part of the United States led to the failure to ratify the treaty. Yet, the increasing exploitation of the oceans and their resources raises the question as to whether some international coordinated effort is needed to protect marine resources in order to meet everyone's interests.

* * *

In a speech in August 1967 before the General Assembly, Ambassador Arvid Pardo of Malta requested that the United Nations reconsider the existing marine legal regime. Pardo also recommended that the United Nations establish international control over the mineral wealth of the seabed and ocean floor in order to regulate competing national claims to those natural resources. The ocean resources, he suggested, should be treated as the "common heritage of mankind" to be regulated by an international organization. The full adoption of this proposal by the United Nations would mean that the seabed could not be appropriated by any state, would be reserved exclusively for peaceful purposes, and would be exploited primarily in the interests of humankind with special regard to the needs of developing countries.

There are a number of reasons why countries sought to claim sovereignty over ocean resources. The years following World War II saw an increase in offshore drilling capabilities, an improved ability to locate, catch, and process fish, and the beginnings of technology to recover manganese nodules lying on the deep-seabed floor. In part, it was the newfound ability to recover the oil under the continental shelf that spurred the Truman proclamations. These proclamations asserted the right of the United States to the resources beneath the continental shelf and created a national fishing conservation zone. Because the jurisdictional claims of the Truman administration were based simply on "physical adjacency and anticipation of use,"[1] they provided a justification for other nations to make broader claims. Between 1945 and 1950 thirty nations asserted rights to the continental shelf or some form of contiguous zone. Many of these claims were made by Central and South American countries, which created maritime or national zones as wide as 200 miles.

The desire to protect coastal waters also grew out of developments in the distant-water fishing industry. Because the yields of U.S. coastal fishermen could be threatened by the Japanese and Russian fishing fleets, and those of South American fishermen by U.S. and other fleets, extending sovereignty to the ocean was seen as a means to conserve and manage this exhaustible resource. Finally, the technological possibility of recovering resources lying on the deep-seabed floor placed a new issue on the international agenda. Primarily in Pacific waters, 13,000-to-16,500-feet deep, lie polymetallic nodules containing commercially valuable concentrations of manganese, nickel, copper, and cobalt.[2] New recovery technology raised the question of resource ownership. For those countries with the potential to bring the nodules to the surface, some form of national jurisdiction over the seabed would guarantee an environment stable enough to make the necessary investments.

Advances in technology and demands due to growing populations and rising incomes, increased nationalist claims to marine resources. These claims brought coastal and distant-water fishermen into conflict and engendered complex management and protection problems. The assertion of exclusive fishing zones by South American countries, for example, was partly prompted by the perception that the distant-water fleets of the United States were taking advantage of the resources of the developing countries. There were also political and strategic reasons for advancing nationalist claims. The dramatic increase in demand for oil and critical minerals drove nations to protect whatever reserves were found off their coasts. Extending national jurisdiction over these resources was justified in light of these security concerns. For some states, extending national jurisdiction was seen as a way of protecting the nation's interests from real and imagined foreign intervention.

The issues that came to dominate the law of the sea negotiations developed in a variety of forums. Claims were often unilaterally made, to which other nations often unilaterally responded. For example, through the 1950s and 1960s Latin American countries sometimes attempted to enforce their claims to the fishing rights off their coasts by seizing U.S. fishing boats. The U.S. government responded by compensating U.S. fishermen, pressuring Latin American governments, and appealing to regional forums. An attempt to redress the erosion of the freedom of the seas regime was made on a global scale at the 1958 and 1960 UNCLOS conferences.

In 1958, at UNCLOS I, 700 delegates from eighty-six countries came to an agreement over four conventions. The Convention on the Continental Shelf essentially codified the Truman proclamations. It established the rights of a coastal state over the natural resources of the continental shelf out to 200-meters depth or beyond "to where the depth of the super-adjacent waters admits of the exploration of the natural resources of said areas." The conference also arrived at a Convention on the Territorial Sea and Contiguous Zone, a Convention on the High Seas, and a Convention on Fisheries. A substantial number of states ratified the conventions establishing resource rights to the continental shelf, 12-mile contiguous zones, and reaffirming the freedom of navigation, fishing, and overflight in the high seas. Fewer nations ratified the convention attempting to balance the interest of coastal and distant-water fishing. However, the work of UNCLOS I was largely incomplete because it failed to establish the breadth of the territorial sea and the related fishing zone, to delineate the limits of the continental shelf, and to consider the issues of the deep seabed. Nevertheless, the work of UNCLOS I was a success compared with the results of UNCLOS II.

The closest UNCLOS II came to accomplishing something meaningful was in setting the width of the territorial sea. However, the conference fell one vote short of establishing a 6-mile territorial sea and a 6-mile fisheries zone. Only two resolutions were passed: one to encourage technical assistance on fishing for developing countries and another to fund and publish the records of the conference.

Overall, these conferences did not successfully deal with the breakdown of the freedom of the seas regime. Maritime states (those states that can be considered sea powers and that have an interest in maintaining high-seas freedoms) were generally dissatisfied by the lack of an international agreement on the territorial sea. Guaranteed passage through the straits was a primary concern, since increases in the width of the territorial sea could close off international straits and restrict naval mobility. Developing states were dissatisfied by the conferences' failure to recognize a 12-mile territorial zone and a fishing zone. Latin American countries in particular considered both demands as prophylactics against the continued encroachment by the industrialized countries as necessary to establish strong, independent economies. Finally, because newly independent African states had not participated in the conferences, questions were raised regarding the legitimacy of the conferences' results.

The General Assembly decided to convene a Third United Nations Law of the Sea Conference to consider not only seabed resources but also the width of the territorial sea, freedom of movement through international straits, management of fishing on the high seas, regulation of marine scientific research, and protection of the marine environment.

DISCUSSION QUESTIONS

1. *Had global conditions regarding oceans and the exploitation of marine resources fundamentally changed to the degree that the cosmopolitan could argue for the application of a standard of justice in international relations?*

2. *Do the outcomes of UNCLOS I and UNCLOS II prove the moral skeptic to be correct in that self-interest governs relations among states?*
3. *What distributive issues did UNCLOS I and II leave unaddressed?*
4. *How are some of the issues addressed by UNCLOS III different from those raised by previous conferences on the sea?*
5. *Why does the deep seabed pose special problems for the international community? Are the Antarctica and the management of the atmosphere analogous cases?*

PARTICIPANTS, POWER, AND INTERESTS

More that 160 countries took part in the negotiations of UNCLOS III, dividing themselves into several overlapping groups. These groups included countries interested in traditional issues of maritime law, for example, width of territorial sea, nature of contiguous zone, extent of high-seas freedoms. Territorialists, such as Latin American countries, were interested in claiming a 200-mile territorial sea. Other countries sought sovereign rights to the continental shelf when the shelf extended beyond the 200-mile zone. Some countries sought a 200-mile economic zone, although countries with no access to the oceans or those whose access was to a resource-poor or narrow continental shelf wanted a mechanism for the equitable distribution of the resources.

Extensive differences also emerged over the nontraditional issue of deep-seabed mining. Those countries with the technology to mine wanted to establish a regime that was most conducive to bringing the minerals up to the surface. Those countries that were exporting the minerals wished to establish a regime that would either forestall or impose production limits on seabed mining. These limits would ensure that deep-seabed mining did not prove too competitive with their land-based production. A further faction consisted of states that consumed, or were not importers of, the minerals found in the nodules. Like the technologically advanced states, these countries had an interest in mining the minerals in the most effective way possible. Other states that possessed deposits of these nodules near or in possible contiguous zones wanted their interests protected by an international regime.

Perhaps the most cohesive faction was the "Group of 77" countries that brought a set of ideological and economic interests to the conference. The Group of 77 was made up of developing countries that helped to formulate and supported the adoption by the United Nations General Assembly of the New International Economic Order Program. The Group of 77 argued that existing international trade, energy, and financial regimes either inadvertently or intentionally discriminated against developing countries in a variety of ways. The interests of these countries lay in establishing a regime that would control mining and divide the revenues equitably among nations. Without the regime, the Group of 77 believed that the goals of developing countries, to modernize and industrialize, would be impeded.

The Conflict of U.S. Interests

From the U.S. perspective the complexity of the negotiations, given the range of international factions, was compounded by the extent of domestic divisions within the United States. Significant bureaucratic divisions within the executive branch included the departments of Defense, State, Interior, and Commerce. All of these departments had an interest in how the U.S. negotiating stance was formulated. The primary interest of the Department of Defense was to preserve the mobility of the navy by ensuring high-seas freedoms and guaranteeing transit through straits. The State Department wanted the negotiations to ensure good international relations and arrive at a mutually acceptable treaty. Securing oil rights to a broadly defined continental shelf was the Interior Department's hope, and Commerce sought to protect fishing rights and establish access to the deep seabed for U.S. companies.

Congress also sought to influence the negotiations. For example, Senate committees on interior and insular affairs and the subcommittee on the outer continental shelf applied political pressure on successive administrations to develop positions favorable to their constituencies. These constituencies included lobbying groups from the oil and mining industries. All had vested interests in a new regime.

As a nation with thousands of miles of coastline and valuable fishing and oil resources located above and below a wide continental shelf, it appeared that U.S. interests would be served by greater jurisdiction over ocean space. The oil industry advanced the most insistent claims for extending national jurisdiction over the continental shelf. It argued that exclusive access to the oil under the continental shelf was vital to national security. Without the 200-mile exclusive economic zone, foreign oil companies were free to come and drill. The oil industry was willing to compromise free transit in order to obtain exclusive rights to the oil. Similarly, coastal fishermen pressed for greater jurisdiction to protect fishing stocks off U.S. coasts.

For the navy, any extension of national jurisdiction over water was a potential threat—either in its direct consequences or as a precedent—to its mission. Defense Department officials repeatedly made the case that if territorial seas were extended only 12 nautical miles, "Traditional activities in 116 international straits less than 24 miles in width could be restricted."[3] Preserving naval mobility required that high seas freedom in the straits be protected worldwide. Furthermore, the navy sought to prevent "creeping jurisdiction,"[4] by which high-seas freedoms could be eroded in a piecemeal but very steady fashion. The navy viewed any jurisdiction as a very slippery slope because claims incrementally extending the jurisdiction of coastal powers could be used as precedent for more expansive claims. Consequently, the Department of Defense favored not only free transit through straits but also restrictions on economic claims to offshore areas, a narrow definition of the continental shelf, and an international seabed regime. Whatever deterred further national extensions was seen as good for U.S. maritime interests.

Distant-water fishermen also saw the extension of coastal state jurisdiction as a threat to their livelihood. They feared a regime would legitimize the types of seizures that had beset U.S. fishermen off South American coasts in the 1950s and 1960s. Finally, the hard minerals industry, which gained influence during the second part of the conference when deep-seabed mining was discussed, believed in the potential of mining the ocean floor. It lobbied U.S. negotiators to advance the least intrusive international regime possible, a position that resonated most strongly in the Reagan administration.

DISCUSSION QUESTIONS

1. *What ethical framework most closely approximates the position taken by the Group of 77?*
2. *How do the various ends particular nations and groups pursue determine the kind of distribution patterns they want to see established in a new marine regime?*
3. *Dividing up the seas, in the same way that land is divided up among nations, would allow countries to extend their borders across the ocean until they met the jurisdiction of another country. Is this type of enclosure of the seas the most just way of addressing the various claims to ocean resources?*
4. *Does the lack of access to a resource-rich continental shelf entitle a land-locked country to an equitable distribution of resources by countries that do have access to broad and resource-rich continental shelves?*
5. *Whose interests should the U.S. negotiators serve? What is a just representation of the various domestic interests by U.S. negotiators at the negotiating table?*

PRENEGOTIATIONS

The Nixon administration's decision to submit a proposal to the United Nations Seabed Committee in August 1970 was done with an understanding of the nature of U.S. interests and with a formulated idea of what the general form of the treaty should be. Through the 1960s, both the United States and the Soviet Union tried to keep the seabed issue apart from the other issues. As late as 1969 the superpowers voted against a General Assembly Resolution calling for a law of the sea conference.

The Nixon proposal implied that the United States was willing not only to negotiate a law of the sea treaty but also to negotiate a comprehensive treaty. The Nixon administration called for the renunciation of national claims to cease beyond the depth of 200 meters, the creation of a trusteeship zone in which the coastal state would have access to resources at the continental margin, the development of international machinery to "authorize and regulate exploration and use of seabed resources,"[5] and a 12-mile limit for territorial seas on the condition that "free transit through international straits was guaranteed." The proposal's immediate effect was to infuse new life into the United Nation's efforts to negotiate a new international regime. But the proposal also unleased a wave of domestic opposition and resistance, giving birth to new interest groups that would become significant as negotiations proceeded.

Once the decision was made to negotiate a comprehensive law of the sea treaty, three committees were established to deal with the issues. Committee I was primarily concerned with issues surrounding the use of the deep seabed. It sought to address the question of who should have rights to mine the seabed and under what terms. Committee II was charged with drawing up that part of the treaty dealing with, and defining the traditional subjects of, maritime law and was to establish the rights and responsibilities regarding the territorial sea, international straits, the contiguous zone, the continental shelf, fishing, and the high seas. Committee III dealt with regulations regarding scientific aspects of the ocean; pollution, scientific research, and the transfer of marine technology.

The negotiations themselves were to proceed on the basis of consensus, and voting was to serve only as a final resort. The UNCLOS III procedural rules set out the rationale for consensus:

> Bearing in mind that the problems of ocean space are closely related and need to be examined as a whole and the desirability of adopting a convention on the Law of the Sea which will ensure the widest possible acceptance, the Conference should make every effort to reach an agreement on substantive matters by way of consensus a n d   t h e r e should be no voting on such matters until all efforts at consensus have been exhausted.[6]

To facilitate this consensus, committee chairpersons were given wide latitude to modify the texts based on how talks were proceeding. The power of committee chairpersons combined with the consensus rule gave the committee members greater maneuvering room to develop ideas, linkages, and agreements that would have been stifled by the public and more official mechanisms of voting. The primary disadvantage to moving by consensus was that it was a slow and tedious process. Although giving greater power to committee chairpersons mitigated this difficulty, it created the potential problem of chairpersons monopolizing power.

DISCUSSION QUESTIONS

1. *What are the advantages and disadvantages of negotiating a comprehensive treaty as opposed to a series of treaties on different issue areas?*
2. *Which approach is more likely to result in a fairer distribution of rights to usage of ocean resources?*
3. *Which ethical framework comes closest to endorsing the consensus model? Which is farthest from it?*

THE NEGOTIATING PROCESS

In 1974, the United States conditionally accepted the idea of a 200-mile economic zone, and, in 1976, it dramatically extended its jurisdiction over fishing rights. Although freedom of navigation was preserved in this economic zone, the United States had clearly backtracked from its maritime interests. The end of the Vietnam War and concern about getting embroiled in other Third World conflicts weakened the navy's argument that it needed to maintain global commitments. Equally important, the Arab oil boycott of 1973 increased the importance of U.S. development of coastal oil reserves; national jurisdiction, in some ways, no longer seemed to be such a bad idea.

The U.S. retreat from a strong maritime position appeared to open the way for a broader agreement. The United Kingdom and the Soviet Union also accepted the 200-mile economic zone. Although the landlocked states were obviously unhappy, the developing countries considered this shift by the maritime powers to be a victory. But with this gain there were other setbacks. Nations located on straits sought to regulate closely the types of ships they would allow to pass. Landlocked and geographically disadvantaged states continued to demand access to the sea and its economic resources. The precise nature of the economic zone (was it to be governed by the conventions of the high seas, territorial seas, or was it to bear a unique set of rights and obligations), the rights with regard to the territorial sea, and the extent and definition of the continental shelf (some of which extended beyond the 200-mile economic zone) had yet to be defined and agreed upon.

Committee II: Negotiating the Maritime Issues

Recognizing that the developing countries were not a monolithic bloc, the United States (as well as other countries) worked with the representatives of different groups of nations to achieve acceptable compromises. For example, the United States obtained free transit on the straits and overflight rights by dividing the coastal-straits from the archipelagic-straits nations. The United States made concessions to Fiji, Indonesia, Malaysia, Mauritius, and the Philippines in exchange for their support of U.S. claims for free passage through and above straits. "The final archipelago articles (Pt. 11, Arts. 117-130) were extremely generous to the archipelago group. Archipelagic states were allowed to draw straight baselines linking the outermost points of their outermost islands and drying reefs to enclose archipelagic waters."[7] This negotiating bloc isolated the coastal-straits nations who did not want to concede free transit and overflight rights over straits in exchange for a 200-mile economic zone.

The U.S. position on free transit, supported by the Soviet Union, included all types of surface ships, submarines, and aircraft. Some states objected to the inclusion of oil tankers and nuclear-powered vessels. The United States insisted that unrestricted passage of oil tankers was critical to national security and that it would not accept any treaty that restricted the transit of ships up to the 12-mile limit and within the limit through international straits. By the time the second session was held in Geneva in 1975, developing countries were beginning to view the intransigence of coastal-straits nations with suspicion. The developing countries recognized the advantage of free transit as they themselves were dependent upon the straits for oil import or export.

Committee II also resolved problems concerning the continental shelf by providing for international revenue sharing between the area where the 200-mile economic zone ended and where the shelf ended. Other proposals called for limiting territorial water to 12 miles, extending resource rights for coastal states to 200 miles, assuring freedom of navigation, and establishing the right to sue a state that interfered with any of these rights. Each point represented significant benefits to both the maritime and coastal interests of the United States.

U.S. successes in Committee II can be attributed not only to a softening of the U.S. maritime position and the exploitation of particular cleavages but also to a pliancy in the developing countries' position. The willingness of the developing countries to accept many of these maritime freedoms stemmed from a perception that the negotiations of Committee II could ultimately be linked to Committee I negotiations. In other words, they believed that cooperation with the industrialized countries on maritime matters could result in a regime favorable to their own deep-seabed interests.

Committee III: Compromises

Committee III, charged with regulating scientific research, also confronted conflicting maritime and coastal interests. Maritime nations generally resisted, although coastal nations demanded, greater environmental control and regulation. Given its coastal interests, the United States sided with the environmentalists, but because of its maritime interests it ultimately argued for minimal powers of enforcement for coastal states. Among the industrialized states, Canada pushed hardest for the development of international environmental law.

Differing positions on the environment, however, did not create a clean maritime/coastal split among nations. Some developing coastal states (for example, India, Indonesia, and Kenya) strongly favored greater power to the coastal state. Other developing coastal nations believed that economic development should take priority over environmental regulations. The desire for unimpeded economic development and navigation, on the one hand, and for greater coastal control, on the other, eventually split the Group of 77.

Nevertheless, negotiators continually attempted to balance the enforcement and regulatory powers of the coastal nations against the navigational concerns of the maritime nations. Under the freedom of the seas regime, maritime interests had been advantaged: Only the flag state (the state in which a ship is registered) was authorized to enforce pollution controls. By 1979, a formula more favorable to the coastal nations developed. Under the treaty, the flag state retained responsibility for punishing violators, but the coastal states could inspect, initiate proceedings against, and detain ships that had transgressed environmental standards. The standards, however, had to be internationally acceptable so as to avoid unduly burdening navigation. Consequently, they did not apply to any warship, vessel, or aircraft used for governmental, noncommercial service. Thus, overall, the maritime states were successful in fending off any environmental regime that accorded significant power to the coastal states.

In dealing with the issue of how states should conduct scientific research in the exclusive 200-mile economic zones, Committee III was split between the industrialized and developing nations. The central goal of the industrialized nations was to secure the right to conduct research in the 200-mile zone with as few regulations as possible. Developing coastal nations wanted all research to be done with the consent of the coastal state. Their reasoning, according to Canadian lawyer Leonard Legault, was that the current regime of research freedom had not benefited the developing countries:

Because they understand the economic uses of marine scientific research, they view freedom of research as a pathway for the erosion of their sovereign rights over the resources of the economic zone . . . Perhaps they forget that you do not gain freedom in one field by denying it in another. But I am sure they are right in saying that "pure" research is a rare thing: Einstein and a bit of chalk—but that led to the atomic bomb. Knowledge is power, they say: and who can disagree? How, they ask, can they manage their resources if those wishing to exploit them know more about them than they do? How can they bring about a real transfer of technology if they cannot participate meaningfully in all research within their economic zone? And how can they truly participate without control?[8]

Even given their differences, all parties agreed that consent to do research within the territorial sea must be obtained from the coastal nation. The problem was how much control a coastal state should have over the nature and extent of the research. A large group of developing coastal states argued for the right to control completely all marine research in the economic zone. The second group consisted of states (for example, Australia, Canada, Ireland, and Mexico) that essentially agreed with the developing coastal states but argued that the research should not be unreasonably restricted. The third negotiating position (held, for example, by Denmark, East Germany, Poland, the Soviet Union, and the United Kingdom) argued that consent should be a prerequisite only when the research related to the exploitation of minerals. This position, of course, would permit research related to military considerations. The fourth position, held by the United States and some Western European nations, held out for the least intrusive regime possible—one that would guarantee the widest sphere of research freedom.

Under the treaty, research could be conducted within the 200-mile zone only with the explicit or tacit consent of the relevant nation. To obtain such consent, researchers would be required to explain the project, give the host nation a right to participate, and agree to make their findings known to the host. If the host nation did not reply to the proposal within four months, researchers could assume that the coastal nation tacitly consented to the project.

Committee I: Defining the "Common Heritage of Mankind"

The most difficult negotiations were those of Committee I concerned with how to distribute rights to mine minerals beyond the 200-mile limit. Both economic and ideological issues divided the industrialized nations and the developing countries on this issue. Economic questions centered on the most appropriate regime for mining minerals in international waters. Because of the level of technology, investment, and risk involved, only a few industrialized countries could mine the seabed. An international regime needed to be established that would provide incentives for the developed nations (and private companies) to mine the seabed but that would also guarantee access by developing countries. Distributive questions concerning the nature of ownership of the seabed minerals needed to be addressed. Did they, as the developing countries maintained, belong to everyone or, as the United States asserted, to no one? What did the phrase, "the common heritage of mankind" truly mean?

The United States wanted unencumbered access to the minerals on the ocean floor. In particular, the United States sought access to the strategic minerals of manganese and cobalt, which are found in great abundance on the seabed and which are necessary for steel production. The fact that the United States imports virtually all of its manganese and cobalt from a few land-based sources, and the possibility that the Soviet Union and South Africa would be the major producers of manganese by the turn of the century, meant that future access to supplies could not be guaranteed. Given this dependence, the United States wanted any law of the sea treaty to ensure the availability of the seabed. Beginning with the August 1970 draft treaty, the United States agreed to the creation of an international authority that would license mining by both private companies and the states. The very existence of such an authority was a concession by the United States because it presented at least a potential obstacle to private companies' developing the seabed. To guard against undue international control that could stifle private mining, the United States insisted that the industrially advanced states be granted greater powers, including the right to veto the authority's decisions. Only with this control, U.S. negotiators argued, would private companies feel they could justify the costs and risks associated with deep-seabed mining.

The developing countries disagreed. They countered that if the seas were truly "the common heritage of mankind," a powerful international authority would be needed to represent the interests of all nations equitably. The right of access to seabed mining should be within the exclusive control of the international authority. The seabed authority, as proposed by the United States, would be merely a means of guaranteeing access to the nodules to those who had the technology. The developing countries wanted an authority (subsequently labeled the Enterprise) with supranational powers, including the ability to exploit the nodules and distribute revenues. Power within the Enterprise would be equally distributed, reflecting the fact that the seabed belonged to all. According to Arvid Pardo:

> The oceans involve the interests of all, and all must therefore work together to establish an equitable regime beneficial to all. Present law of the sea based on freedom and sovereignty is being rapidly eroded by technology and events and is, in any case, incapable of providing a lasting framework for the beneficial use of ocean space under present conditions. A new basis for a new regime must be created.[9]

The issue of ownership of seabed minerals exacerbated the dispute between the developing countries and the industrialized nations, with developing countries' delegates arguing that the nodules lying on the ocean floor were not within any nation's jurisdiction and thus belonged to all humankind. Because everyone owned the minerals, they continued, only an international authority committed to distributing equitably the revenues from mining should be allowed to operate. An individual state or private mining company mining the nodules would, in effect, be stealing them from their rightful owners—the rest of the world. At the very least, the international authority should control through contracts who mined, how much they mined, and how the revenues were distributed. At the most, such an authority would directly undertake the mining.

The developing countries also pointed out that a strong international authority had certain political advantages. It would be heavily supported by the developing, landlocked, and geographically disadvantaged nations. If successful, such a formula could also provide a stable environment for mining and begin to meet the developing states' claims to distributive justice. The developing countries argued that the poorest countries ought to be the recipients of the benefits derived from mining the "common heritage of mankind." Finally, a strong seabed authority would provide a precedent for peacefully and cooperatively dealing with common areas and resources in the future.

The practical difficulties of enacting this formula of the authority were enormous. If the authority itself was to engage in mining, how would it obtain the means to do so from the industrialized nations that had the technology and capital? Without proper incentives, industrialized nations might be reluctant to participate and could foreclose the authority's success. The United States in particular was reluctant to agree to such a formula. Opponents of the treaty in the United States feared that establishing a strong international authority would serve as an unfortunate precedent. In the view of Northcutt Ely:

> Once the principle is conceded that an agency of the United Nations shall have the inherent power to deny, grant, condition and revoke a nation's power to use the bed of the sea for production of minerals, it becomes difficult to say why, on principle, the international authority should not have similar competence to grant or deny use of the seabed for all purposes, including peaceful military uses, and, indeed, to grant or deny use of the water column itself.[10]

The industrialized nations argued that the nodules were not owned by everyone but by no one; because no one owned the nodules, they were available to anyone who could take them. To legitimize their position, they drew on John Locke's argument that the acquisition of private property in a "state of nature" is created by labor. If the developing countries lacked the resources to develop the nodules, they could not own them. In other words, the seabed was *res nullius*, it belonged to no one and therefore was open to claim by anyone who worked for it.

There were a number of formulas that could reflect the unowned character of the seabed. The least intrusive regime would be an unregulated market. Companies and states simply mined where they wanted. Under this regime, it would be the miners' responsibility to protect their claims. A somewhat more intrusive, but still acceptable, regime would allow mining either under the auspices of a flag state or under a larger regional regime in which like-minded states guaranteed each other's claims (a formula eventually advocated under the name of the mini-treaty solution). In 1970, the United States suggested perhaps the least intrusive international regime, which remained true to the spirit of the seabed as *res nullius*. Under this system, mining would be left to the initiative of the individual state or corporation. The miner would stake a claim, register it with the international authority, and expect that his claim would be respected by others.

According to the industrialized states, the advantages of a weak authority were numerous. Supply and demand would be an incentive to create an efficient, international authority to establish production limits and prices. Such a regime would not require massive capital and technology transfers. The market would decide when, where, and how much to mine. If mining became economically feasible, those states with the capability to mine would mine. Because of these efficiencies, the world would benefit from the increased availability of these minerals, which, under a more intrusive and cumbersome regime would remain, they argued, on the bottom of the ocean.

The disadvantage of the free market approach was that it did not address many of the developing countries' grievances on distributive issues. More important, the demand for a weak seabed authority could put other treaty goals of the industrialized maritime powers at risk. The developing countries had linked gains in Committee I negotiations to concessions in Committee II negotiations. The refusal to create a strong seabed authority could jeopardize the protection of maritime freedoms. (The developing countries wanted to convince the industrialized world that "navigation" could be only secured with "nodules.") Furthermore, if a free market approach generated little international support, mining operations could be threatened. Without a stable international regime that held mining claims to the deep-seabed as legitimate, companies would be unwilling to risk the millions of dollars necessary to proceed with mining.

In spite of these risks, the United States envisioned an authority that could not exact payments from companies, license mining firms, require technology transfers, or set prices and production levels. In short, the United States conceived of a regime in which it possessed sufficient influence to guarantee its interests. The developing countries clung to the opposing view on each of these issues, and a stalemate ensued.

DISCUSSION QUESTIONS

1. *Is one conception of property more relevant to the distributive issues at hand than another?*
2. *What would it mean for the international authority to control mining rights and de facto own the deep-seabeds?*
3. *Is the supply and demand of the marketplace, as the United States believed, an adequate way of deciding distributive issues such as the exploitation of nodules and the management of marine fish stocks? Is it a fair way of doing it?*
4. *What kinds of obligations do the industrialized countries have to share their technology to mine the deep-seabeds as well as to conduct marine research with developing countries?*

NEGOTIATING THE FINAL TREATY

In 1976, Secretary of State Henry Kissinger offered a number of compromises that became known as the parallel system. From the U.S. perspective, these compromises were quite extensive. The largest concession accorded the Enterprise a right to mine, alongside of companies' and states' rights to mine. The United States did not believe that the Enterprise should exclusively hold this right; private companies and individual states should also be allowed access to seabed minerals. Hence the parallel nature of the formula. Kissinger's formula also offered a system for choosing and developing the parallel mines, known as the banking sites; the suggestion of transferring technology and production controls; an agreement to finance the authority, and the safety valve of periodic review. What remained at issue was political control of the authority and the details of the financial and production arrangements.

Although the U.S. position had softened, the developing states of the Group of 77 felt that the Kissinger formula demanded even greater concessions on their part. The parallel system itself, by guaranteeing access to companies and individual nations, was seen as a violation of the "common heritage of mankind" principle. In response, the Kissinger proposal was subsequently and single-handedly revised by Committee Chairperson Paul Engo from Cameroon. These revisions, involving issues of technology transfer, financial liability of contractors, production limitations, voting power, and regulation of scientific research, mollified the Group of 77 but upset the United States and led U.S. Ambassador Elliot Richardson to call for a review of the substance and procedure of the conferences. After further negotiations, which reduced the power of committee chairpersons to revise the text, the essence of a bargain had emerged in which the United States (and other industrialized nations) would make concessions on the mining issues in exchange for developing countries' concessions on freedom of navigation.

The formula of the parallel system allowed negotiators to work rapidly toward closure during the 1979 and 1980 treaty sessions. Although negotiations continued to be difficult, the pace of agreement and compromise accelerated. On the vexing issue of technology transfer, for example, the treaty was altered to oblige the transfer of technology to the Enterprise only if the technology was unavailable on the market, while sections requiring the transfer of technology to developing countries remained. On the critical issue of voting procedures, the parties agreed that different issues would require different majorities. Procedural issues would be decided simply by majority vote, and more substantive issues would require greater majorities or a consensus. Other compromises resulted in agreement or near agreement on scientific research and production controls.

By fall 1980, a draft of the treaty had been endorsed by Elliot Richardson and most other representatives. The treaty contained much that the United States sought, in particular, agreements that codified the doctrine of freedom of the high seas. Even in creating a 200-mile economic zone, the treaty preserved high-seas freedoms. Aside from the 200-mile zone, the treaty established a 12-mile territorial sea, a 24-mile contiguous zone, and a continental shelf boundary that extended at least 200 miles from the shore baseline. By creating two legal rights of passage the treaty also attempted to ally the concerns of maritime states whose military and commercial interests were threatened by the extension of the territorial sea. In archipelagic waters, states were guaranteed essentially the same right of innocent passage allowed in territorial waters. In passage through straits, freedom of navigation and overflight was guaranteed for continuous and expeditious transit. In both cases, the relevant states, along with international organizations, could propose sea-lane and traffic regulations.

The regime established to govern the seabed was based largely on the idea of the parallel system. The treaty described an International Seabed Authority to include an assembly, council, and the Enterprise. All parties to the treaty would also be members of the assembly. Each state would have one vote in setting general policy, electing members of the council, establishing the Enterprise Governing Board, and distributing the financial benefits of exploiting the seabed. As mentioned earlier, depending on the nature of the issue at hand, different decisions would require different majorities.

The council would be composed of thirty-six members; large investors, major consumers, large land-based exporters of minerals, and other special-interest categories would receive greater representation. Remaining members were to be chosen on the basis of geographic location. The council's purpose was to establish rules for governing the seabed system, to adopt recommendations from an Economic Planning Commission and a Legal and Technical Commission, to select applicants for mining licenses, and to arrange the funding for the authority and the Enterprise. The actual mining, transportation, processing, and marketing of minerals recovered from the seabed devolved to the Enterprise. A fifteen-member governing board and director general would control the Enterprise, and ensuing profits would be treated as "the common heritage of mankind."

- A state, company, consortium, or the Enterprise applies to exploit a worthwhile tract of the seabed. (All private miners must be sponsored by a state that has ratified the treaty. Every seabed tract to be mined must be large enough to support two mining operations.)
- Once the Council approves the application, half the tract is given to the applicant, who now has an exclusive right to mine the area (subject to production limitations on the particular minerals). Half the tract is designated a reserved site, which can now be mined by the Enterprise if it develops plans that are technologically and financially sound.
- If the Enterprise decides not to mine the site, other states or private actors can apply to exploit the tract.

Proponents of the treaty argued that the convention assured access to miners, guaranteed a fair return given the risks involved, and protected against the arbitrary power of the authority. Equally important, the treaty promised to improve relations between the United States and the developing countries. Although the treaty contained provisions the United States did not like, especially concerning the mining of the seabed, Richardson and others argued that these concessions, embodied in Kissinger's formula of the parallel system, were trivial compared with the gains the treaty would bring about and that the concessions were necessary to "buy" other states' acceptance of points in the treaty that were important to the United States.

At this point, the newly elected Reagan administration transformed the closure phase of negotiations in an attempt to work out a new formula. On 2 March 1981, the administration decided to conduct a policy review of the law of the sea negotiations. The review was concluded and made public on 29 January 1982. Although the administration found much of the treaty acceptable, particularly the sections on freedom of navigation and coastal rights, it rejected the provisions on deep-seabed mining. The existing provisions would deter the exploitation of the seabed, officials argued, and would give too much power to the developing countries, require U.S. technology transfer, and set a bad precedent by giving an international agency so much authority. The administration proposed that the Enterprise, in essence, be transformed into a claims registry, that the United States have much greater voting power, and that the treaty rid itself of its "offensive" (socialist) ideological nature.

The Group of 77 rejected the Reagan proposals, arguing that they were a direct repudiation of the parallel system and gave full power to private companies and states at the expense of the Enterprise. Once again, the developing countries asserted, the principle of "the common heritage of mankind" had been subverted. To bridge the gap, "Good Samaritan" countries proposed several changes that increased U.S. influence in the authority and weakened the provisions of technology transfer. Many of these proposals, over the objections of some developing countries, were then incorporated into the treaty.

Despite the compromises, the Reagan administration remained dissatisfied. Voting power in the authority, for example, would not reflect the financial support that the West would contribute. Moreover, the United States was not assured a seat in the executive council, which would be responsible for implementing the authority's day-to-day decisions. Although the final negotiating sessions had guaranteed representation to the largest consumer of deep-seabed minerals, Washington feared that the Soviet Union could qualify for such a position, depending on how "largest consumer" was defined. The administration argued that the convention did not assure the United States the kind of control over decision making consummate with its financial contribution or interests.

The United States further contended that the establishment of production limitations to protect land-based producers and the authority's ability to tax private production were unreasonable restrictions on its ability to access and develop the strategic minerals lying on the deep-seabed. The administration also argued that the idea of creating banking sites and guaranteeing access and technology to the Enterprise provided an unfair competitive advantage over private operations. For example, a private company would be unable to rely on defense-related technology that was nontransferable under U.S law. Consequently, nontransferable technology that was integral to a private mining operation would have to be either made available (contrary to U.S. law) or not used in production (handicapping the operation).[11]

Moreover, U.S. officials argued, because the specific arrangements and ideological nature of the International Seabed Authority would deter economic development, the authority would ultimately threaten U.S. economic and strategic interests and serve as a precedent for a new "global collectivism." The administration came to believe that any seabed regime exceeding the power of a claim registry—but which it could not adequately control—would be too powerful, too extensive, and too vulnerable to hostile interests.

DISCUSSION QUESTIONS

1. *Why is the parallel system seen by developing countries as a violation of the "common heritage of mankind" principle?*
2. *Are the moral skeptic and the Reagan administration correct in their view that an international authority can never be trusted to be impartial and fair in its decisions?*
3. *In pursuing as much control over the international authority as possible, did the United States harm its interests? Were there some compromises the United States could have made without harming its position?*
4. *Are unilateral alternatives better than a flawed treaty?*

THE VOTE

On 30 April 1982, the United States voted against the final treaty adopted by the third United Nations Conference on the Law of the Sea. The vast majority of the developing countries voted in favor of the treaty, with the Soviet Union and some Western countries abstaining. The United States was the only industrialized nation to vote no. In the final analysis, the refusal to sign the treaty was a tangible demonstration of the Reagan administration's displeasure with any developments that would impede U.S. ability to act independently. Most important, the administration concluded that it need not exchange "navigation" for "nodules" but that it could have both: By relying on customary law (and the power of the U.S. military), freedom of navigation could be maintained. By concluding mini-treaties with the handful of other nations capable of deep-seabed mining and through domestic legislation, the United States could proceed to develop the seabed without the difficulties of working with the authority. The administration rejected the strong international regime and interdependent world that UNCLOS III fostered, considering it an unfavorable precedent and a threat to U.S. freedom of action. (It should be noted, however, that the notion of an unfavorable precedent was not indisputable. For example, Arvid Pardo argued that the treaty, in fact, was a victory for traditional state interests because it now placed 40 percent of ocean space under some form of national control. This 40 percent was significant because of the hydrocarbons, commercially exploitable minerals, and living resources that it contained.) According to James L. Malone, President Reagan's special representative:

Let me state very emphatically that the United States cannot and will not sign the United Nations Convention of the Law of the Sea. The treaty is fatally flawed and cannot be cured. In its present form it presents a serious threat to U.S. vital national interests and, in fact, to global security. Once more, it is inimical to the fundamental principles of political liberty, private property, and free enterprise. The administration firmly believes that those very principles are the key to economic well-being for all countries—developing as well as developed.[12]

The unilateral course set out by the Reagan administration was not without its risks and problems. It was unclear whether the mini-treaty option could offer a secure enough environment for deep-seabed mining. The convention required signatory parties to recognize that the only legitimate regime was the one established by the convention. If the treaty was widely recognized, the U.S. government might have to subsidize mining companies for the political risks of being outside the treaty. It was even possible that to engage effectively in mining, U.S. consortia would have to operate out of signatory countries. By being outside the convention, the United States could poison the well for mining even within a treaty. Because the United States would probably be the largest participant in mining, its unilateral action could make deep-seabed mining too risky both inside and outside the convention.

A second problem was inherent in the belief that the United States could rely on customary law to secure its interests. The argument that the treaty simply codified existing international law ran up against postwar trend of increasing territorial claims by coastal, straits, and archipelagic nations. Indeed, the impetus for an international conference was, in part, the perceived breakdown of customary international law—an uncertainty over exactly what the law prescribed. Furthermore, passage through straits would become dependent on the quality of U.S. bilateral relations with straits nations. If relations with those states soured, the legitimacy of U.S. claims could be diminished by the fact that the treaty made transit right no longer "discretionary, tradable, and disputable." A state that had signed the treaty could always choose to regard it as a package deal, one in which states could not simply pick and choose various articles to follow according to their liking. In the opinion of Leigh S. Ratiner:

Moreover, if the United States stays out of the sea law treaty while most nations join it, we risk conflict over U.S. assertions that we are entitled, without participating in the treaty, to rights embodied in it relate to navigational freedoms, exclusive economic zones, and jurisdiction over our continental shelf, fisheries, pollution control, and the conduct of marine scientific research.[13]

Proponents for signature argued that by staying out of the treaty the United States reduced the number of options available to it when its "rights" become threatened. The notion that the threat or use of force would always, in the end, guarantee U.S. transit rights ignored the possibility that challenges of these rights need not be blatantly provocative. These rights could be eroded by demands for notification, permission, or delay, and challenges could be based on environmental, safety, or resource grounds. The military option simply might not be a proportional or effective response. In addition, the use of force could become prohibitively expensive if transit rights were effectively challenged throughout the world.

DISCUSSION QUESTIONS

1. *Deep-seabed mining may conceivably be addressed by expanding national jurisdiction. Will a similar approach be effective in protecting and conserving the marine environment from pollution and over exploitation? Explain.*
2. *Is a fairer outcome and the interests of individual countries better met through mini-treaties as opposed to a comprehensive one?*
3. *Is the cosmopolitan correct in that global empirical conditions have irrevocably changed the way nations relation and that some global standard of justice is required?*

NOTES

1. Barry Barzan, *Seabed Politics* (New York: Praeger Publishers, 1976), p. 8.
2. *Ibid.*, p. xvii.
3. James K. Sebenius, *Negotiating the Law of the Sea* (Cambridge, Mass.: Harvard University Press, 1984), p. 74.
4. Ann Hollick points out that immediately after World War II, until the late 1960s, "The central problem . . . arising from the exploration of seabed resources, was not that of creeping jurisdiction. Rather it was the need to provide for the accommodation of multiple uses of the ocean environment." The nay assumed that "freedom of the seas could be maintained under an expanding shelf regime." (Hollick, *U.S. Foreign Policy and the Law of the Sea* (Princeton, N.J.: Princeton University Press, 1981), p. 185. This view apparently changed with the Henkin Report (1967) and the Stratton Commission Report (1969). With these reports, the developments in the law of the sea

came to be seen as a "trend" of crisis proportions. The effect of these reports was a redefinition of the problem facing the navy. Instead of accommodating multiple uses of the ocean, the objective was to stop creeping jurisdiction.

5. Finn Laursen, *Superpower at Sea* (New York: Praeger Publishers, 1983), p. 6.

6. Clyde Sanger, *Ordering the Oceans* (Toronto: University of Toronto Press, 1987), pp. 37-38.

7. Hollick, *U.S. Foreign Policy*, p. 305.

8. Sanger, *Ordering the Oceans*, p. 128.

9. Arvid Pardo, "New Institutions for Ocean Space," in Elizabeth Mann Borgese and David Krieger, eds., *The Tides of Change* (New York: Mason Charter, 1975), p. 325.

10. Northcutt Ely, "United States Seabed Minerals Policy," *Natural Resources Lawyer* 4 (July 1971), pp. 614-615.

11. James L. Malone, "Who Needs the Sea Treaty?" *Foreign Policy*, no. 54 (Spring 1984): 55.

12. *Ibid.*, p. 63.

13. Leigh S. Ratiner, "The Costs of American Rigidity," in Bernard H. Oxman, David D. Caron, and Charles L. O. Buderi, eds., *Law of the Sea: U.S. Policy Dilemma* (San Francisco, Calif.: ICS Press, 1983), p. 28.

FURTHER READING ON THE LAW OF THE SEA TREATY

Books

Hollick, Ann. *U.S. Foreign Policy and the Law of the Sea.* Princeton, N.J.: Princeton University Press, 1981.

Hollick, Ann, and Robert E. Osgood. *New Era of Ocean Politics.* Baltimore, Md.: Johns Hopkins University Press, 1974.

Oxman, H. Bernard, David D. Caron, and Charles L. O. Buderi, eds. *Law of the Sea: U.S. Policy Dilemma.* San Francisco: Institute for Contemporary Studies, 1983.

Articles

Bension, Varon, "Ocean Issues on the International Agenda," *Beyond Dependency: The Developing World Speaks Out*, ed. by Guy F. Erb and Valeriana Kallab (Washington, D.C.: Overseas Development Council, 1975), pp. 120-131.

5

DEBT AND SOVEREIGNTY: THE IMF AND NIGERIA, 1983–1986

The attempts on the part of three Nigerian governments to refinance the country's foreign debt raise questions about the central role the International Monetary Fund played in the national economic policies of Nigeria, the IMF's relationship to the World Bank and creditor coalitions, and the Fund's ability to weigh the political sustainability of an agreement, on the one hand, with the economic and political burdens of the agreement for Nigerian society, on the other.

This case study, like the UNCLOS case, examines the ends that drive negotiating positions and questions the fairness of the outcome. As in the UNCLOS case, the negotiations described in this case took place within the framework of an international organization, the IMF. The reasons for the Nigeria-IMF negotiations were quite different from that of the UNCLOS negotiations. In the latter, nations met under the aegis of the United Nations General Assembly to create a new treaty governing the uses of the sea. In the Nigerian case, however, three Nigerian governments negotiated within the parameters of established IMF policies to refinance its external debt.

This chapter is a revised and edited version of the case study by Thomas J. Biersteker, Reaching Agreement with the IMF: The Nigerian Negotiations, 1983-1986, *Pew case study no. 205.*

Debt and Sovereignty

FIGURE 5.1 Nigeria

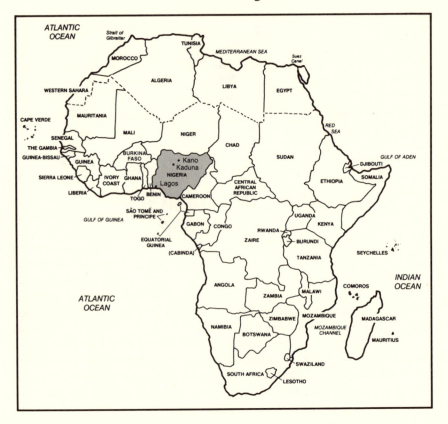

Source: W. Raymond Duncan and Carolyn McGiffert Ekedahl, *Moscow and the Third World Under Gorbachev* (Boulder: Westview Press, 1990), p. 168.

This case study also raises questions about the economic viewpoint the IMF advances in its policy conditions: trade liberalization, payments system, and economic growth. Are the policy prescriptions of the IMF right for a country such as Nigeria? Do the institutional changes they require create more harm than good within a society? In addition to examining the ideological view that guides IMF policy conditions, this case also looks at the issue of political legitimacy. What obligation does the IMF have to respect as much as possible the policymaking autonomy of a government? Not to respect the autonomy of a government is to risk nationalist resentment against the IMF. Moreover, if the IMF does not closely monitor a country's adherence to conditionality, laxness can lead to the perpetuation of existing crony capitalism. Finally, this case study raises questions about the responsibility the IMF has to be sensitive to the political vulnerability of the government. In negotiating with a government, the IMF assumes that it is dealing with a unitary actor. As the Nigeria case shows, a government usually represents many groups within society. Domestic opposition groups can lead to political instability and the withdrawal of a government, such as the Babangida regime, from negotiating an agreement on policy changes.

* * *

Ever since the Organization of Petroleum Exporting Countries (OPEC) first succeeded in raising the price of crude petroleum dramatically in 1973-1974, Nigeria has been a monoculture economy dependent on the export of petroleum. Petroleum proceeds accounted for nearly 95 percent of government revenue during the late 1970s and continued at this level throughout Nigeria's negotiations with the Fund. The petroleum revenues came at a time when Nigeria was already experiencing a decline in agricultural production. Hence, although it created new opportunities, Nigeria's newfound oil income exacerbated a number of other structural problems in the Nigerian economy (such as lagging agricultural performance, inflation, and inequality). The Nigerian economy has long been characterized by high levels of import demand, and the oil income fueled an explosion of consumer-goods imports during the 1970s. It also reinforced the development of a heavily import-intensive manufacturing sector in the country.

When it assumed power from a military administration in October 1979, the civilian regime of President Shehu Shagari faced relatively few external economic constraints. The price for Nigerian crude petroleum was at an all-time high, national oil income had reached unprecedented levels, and prices for Nigeria's major agricultural export (cocoa) were at higher levels than they had been for a decade. The debt/service ratio was an easily manageable 1.5 percent, and foreign exchange reserves increased by a factor of two (to more than $10 billion) during its first year in office.

The Shagari administration was the first elected regime in Nigeria's second republic (civilians had previously ruled the country under a parliamentary system from the time of its independence from Britain in 1960 until a military coup in January 1966). The new constitution that gave birth to Nigeria's second republic was based on a U.S.-style presidential system of governance, with separate legislative, executive, and judicial branches of federal government. Although it was challenged by opposition parties from their bases in state governments, the Shagari administration used Nigeria's new federal system to concentrate political power at the federal level, a concentration that had originally begun under the military during the Nigerian civil war (1967-1970).

The Shagari government was regionally based in northern Nigeria, but it had received strong support in the 1979 elections from the middle-belt and central regions of the country. The ruling National Party of Nigeria (NPN) was widely viewed as a conservative political party that represented the interests of the traditional oligarchy in northern Nigeria, the emerging political and economic class in the north (often referred to as "the Kaduna mafia"), and elements of Nigeria's influential commercial and industrial elite located throughout the country.[1] The NPN was the best funded of the five political parties that competed in the early days of the second republic, and during the 1979 elections it was popularly referred to as the "Naira Party of Nigeria" (a reference to Nigeria's currency, the naira).

During the Shagari government's first two full years in office (in 1980 and 1981), the level of imports into the country more than doubled. The naira was highly overvalued at the time, hence the cost of imported goods was relatively low. To control the volume of imports into the country, the government maintained an elaborate import-licensing scheme in which individual importers received governmental approval (in the form of licenses) to import set quantities of goods. However, the arrangement was fraught with corruption, and the volume of imports was only partially controlled. The new civilian government granted import licenses to its political supporters (licenses that gave them quasi-monopolies to import goods in specific sectors). In return, state and party officials regularly received kickbacks for the granting (or in many instances the direct auctioning) of import licenses.

For a time, the oil income fueled the increased volume of imports. However, existing levels of public expenditure were maintained, the exchange rate appreciated in real terms, and oil production decreased to 69.7 percent of 1980 levels. Petroleum export earnings fell from $25 billion in 1980 to $17.5 billion in 1981. As a result, foreign exchange reserves were drawn down at a rather rapid rate during 1981 to make up for the difference from lost oil revenues. Foreign exchange reserves plummeted from more than $10 billion in 1980, to $4.2 billion in 1981. After a slump in oil exports in the first half of 1981, new external borrowing increased to more than $2 billion.

In September 1981, the Shagari government introduced its first austerity package, designed to cut public expenditure by about $1.6 billion. When the 1982 budget was announced at the end of the year, further cuts (in excess of $3 billion) were announced, along with plans to increase foreign borrowing to make up the balance of payments shortfall. In April 1982, Nigeria drew down its remaining reserves with the IMF, while throughout the year, it continued to increase the level of total external borrowing. The volume of crude petroleum exports continued to drop, and by November, Nigeria was three months in arrears in settling its routine trade debts in foreign exchange. By

TABLE 5.1 Nigeria's Debt Service Ratio (in percent)

Year	Total Debt Service to Export Goods and Services
1975	2.7
1976	3.4
1977	0.8
1978	1.2
1979	1.5
1980	4.2
1981	4.7
1982	16.2
1983	23.7
1984	33.7
1985	33.3
1986	29.8
1987	13.3
1988	27.3

Source: World Debt Tables, second supplement (Washington, D.C.: World Bank, 1989/1990), p. 54.

the end of the year, the fiscal crisis had deepened, and Nigeria's debt service ratio had shot up to 19.3 percent (See Table 5.1).

In February 1983, as the backlog of short-term import debt continued to increase, the Shagari government approached foreign commercial bankers on a $1 billion Eurocredit to help settle its trade arrears. Two months later, in April 1983, the Shagari government initiated negotiations with the IMF.

DISCUSSION QUESTIONS

1. What domestic structures and practices contributed to the economic problems of Nigeria? Can certain individual public officials, for example, Shagari and members of his government, be held responsible?

2. *What international events and structures contributed to Nigeria's worsening economic situation? Can specific institutions and international actors be held accountable?*

3. *Given that the whole country bears the burden of any refinancing, should the Nigerian government be required, for political and moral reasons, to consult with domestic opposition groups and major social/political actors in the country as it decides to enter negotiations with its creditors? Would this strategy correct some of the past domestic practices that have contributed to Nigeria's economic problems?*

4. *Should external agencies such as commercial banks and the IMF consider issues of governance (how people are ruled, how the affairs of a state are administered and regulated) when approached by a country such as Nigeria for financial assistance?*

NEGOTIATING WITH THE IMF

At the outset, Nigeria sought to borrow $2 billion from the Fund, largely to help refinance its trade debt (then estimated to be somewhere between $3 and $5 billion). Because Nigeria had already drawn down its reserve with the Fund, the IMF indicated a number of conditions that would have to be satisfied before it agreed to commit any new funds. The stabilization package the Fund proposed included a devaluation of the naira, a tightening of the money supply, an increase in interest rates, a cutback in recurrent government expenditure, the abolition of a number of consumer subsidies (particularly on petroleum), a wage freeze, and the relaxation of exchange and import controls.

Nigeria's trade debts continued to pile up, and a number of foreign banks began to stop confirming Nigerian letters of credit. With an election scheduled for August 1983, the Shagari government accelerated its efforts to increase the level of external borrowing, and, during the month of June, an agreement was announced between Nigeria and twenty-four international banks. They agreed to refinance $1.6 billion of the country's trade arrears into a three year medium-term loan, with repayment to start after the elections, in January 1984. Nigeria's decision to go to the Fund was described as "helpful" in persuading the banks to negotiate. On the eve of the elections, a World Bank loan of $120 million was announced, with prospects of an increase to $500 million.

President Shagari and the NPN were reelected by a wide margin in August 1983, in elections that were widely viewed as severely rigged.[2] Corruption was nothing new in the history of Nigerian politics, but the NPN had apparently increased it to unprecedented levels. Shortly after the elections, a second refinancing agreement was reached, this time with a total of sixty-five international banks.

Negotiations with the IMF had been continuing throughout this period, and agreement had been reached on a number of conditions. The Nigerians had agreed to reduce government expenditures, increase budgetary discipline, review the feasibility of ongoing projects, reduce the level of subsidies for parastatal firms, end grants to state governments, rationalize customs duties, increase interest rates, reduce money supply, gradually remove fertilizer subsidies, review industrial incentives and policies, promote exports, increase producer prices for agriculture commodities, better manage the external debt, and improve the efficiency of government revenue collection. Despite the progress, however, three major issues blocked an agreement: devaluation, trade liberalization, and an end to petroleum subsidies.

The IMF was primarily concerned with the overvaluation of the naira and the price distortions it produced throughout the economy. The Fund wanted at least a 33 percent devaluation of the currency. The Nigerians countered that a devaluation would have little immediate effect. Because the price of their major export (petroleum) was already denominated in dollars, the Nigerian negotiators contended that a major devaluation would do little to promote exports. Further, they argued that the prices of their other commodity exports were also externally determined (and undergoing a decline to postwar lows at the time). The Shagari government especially feared the consequences a devaluation would have on import prices and the level of domestic inflation.

Trade liberalization was less pressing for the IMF at the outset of the negotiations because the Fund staff thought that the overvalued exchange rate by itself created the principal source of trade protection. The Nigerians argued that the elimination of the trade-licensing scheme could lead to the dumping of goods on the Nigerian market, which could destroy the capacity of the country's infant industries and lead to the potential importation of hazardous substances. The Fund opposed petroleum subsidies, as it did nearly all government price subsidies of any kind. The cut in petroleum subsidies was resisted by Nigerian authorities on two grounds. First, such cuts would produce unacceptable levels of domestic inflation. Second, domestic petroleum prices had become an important symbol of Nigerian wealth. (Also, when higher prices and spot shortages developed within the country in 1974, they helped create a political crisis that undermined the then military government.) From September 1983 to the end of the year, the negotiations between the IMF and Nigeria were stalemated on these three issues.

In his annual budget speech on 29 December, President Shagari announced new austerity measures. Among them were plans for a reduction in the level of imports, a further reduction of the federal budget, and the privatization of a number of state-owned companies. There was no mention of any devaluation. Shagari announced his intention to continue to approach the World Bank and the IMF for structural adjustment and balance-of-payments assistance. Two days later, his government was overthrown by a military coup.

DISCUSSION QUESTIONS

1. *Should the IMF play the critical role of "certifying agent," without whose approval commercial banks, the World Bank, and, to some degree, governments would not loan money to Nigeria?*
2. *Given the unprecedented level of corruption in the Shagari government, should IMF officials have conditioned further refinancing on significant changes in administrative procedures and tighter regulations?*
3. *Is the quality of governance in a country a legitimate concern of any external organization?*
4. *Does an international organization, like the IMF, have a right to impose conditions on a member country especially when those conditions promote policy changes to which officials and experts of the country object?*

RADICAL STABILIZATION WITHOUT THE FUND

When the military returned to power at the beginning of 1984, it faced a number of significant economic problems. Price levels within OPEC had weakened, and, as Nigeria's oil production share continued to decline, its market was increasingly threatened by other producers. Oil income was down, from $25 billion in 1980 to less than $10 billion in 1983. Nigeria's debt service ratio had climbed to 28.3 percent, and its foreign exchange reserves were virtually drained. Domestic inflation was running at a level of 23.2 percent, and industrial production was sharply off.

In his first speech after assuming power, the new head of state, Major General Muhammadu Buhari, emphasized discipline, austerity, self-reliance, and fiscal conservatism—ideas that were to become the basis of his government's policy and its subsequent approach to the Fund. At first, the new regime was greeted with a good deal of popular enthusiasm, coming as it did after what was increasingly perceived as widespread civilian waste and corruption of the preceding four years. At the outset, the new government appeared to be a continuation of the last military government of Generals Muhammed and Obasanjo, the regime that had handed power back to the civilians in 1979. Several members of its governing council had served under

Muhammed and/or Obasanjo (Buhari himself had been petroleum minister), and some of the language of the new government (concerning state management and the economy) was familiar.

However, there was also a fair degree of continuity with the ousted civilian regime. Although it legitimated itself as a corrective regime, intent on cleaning up the economic and political mismanagement of the civilians, the new miliary government was conservative politically, and, like the Shagari government, it too was dominated by northerners. Significantly, a northerner again controlled the distribution of import licenses at the Ministry of Trade. The new regime differed primarily in two major respects: (1) the degree of its distrust of the private sector (which had so effectively penetrated the ousted civilian regime), and (2) the degree of its overt authoritarianism. Nigeria had experienced three successive military governments in its postindependence history (military officers ruled between 1966 and 1979), but the Buhari regime was to prove the most authoritarian.

Shortly after assuming power, the regime launched its "War Against Indiscipline," a national campaign that invoked patriotic appeals in an attempt to increase order and discipline within the country. It also enacted several highly controversial decrees (particularly Decree 2 and Decree 4) that centralized state power to levels unprecedented since the Nigerian civil war (giving it the power to arrest and detain people without trial and effectively censoring Nigeria's lively press).[3] These measures provided the new regime with far greater direction and decisiveness in policymaking. They were also indicative, however, of a tendency within the new leadership to rely on authoritarian measures to bolster its political position, rather than to use ideology to mobilize popular support for its programs.[4]

At the outset, observers at the IMF viewed the new regime with a certain amount of optimism, especially when General Buhari described his approach to Nigeria's accumulated debt: "given prudent management of the existing financial resources, determined substantially to reduce waste . . . it will be possible to clear the accumulated domestic payments arrears, reduce the rising budgetary deficit, and the weak balance of payments deficit." The Fund's hopes for an early resolution to the stalemated talks were short-lived, however. Shortly after his initial speech to the public, Buhari appealed to the IMF for greater understanding of Nigeria's predicament, especially on the question of devaluation. Moreover, he ruled out any reduction of petroleum subsidies (and hence, any increase in domestic fuel prices).

Less than a month after it assumed power, the new military government resumed negotiations (originally begun under Shagari) with a number of Organization for Economic Cooperation and Development (OECD) country export credit agencies under Paris Club auspices. The Paris Club is the forum within which debtor countries negotiate the restructuring of public sector debt with their main creditor governments. It was negotiating a rescheduling of Nigeria's backlog of short-term trade debt, estimated by some observers to have reached $6.7 billion by the time the military had resumed power. There were also disagreements on the amount of interest Nigeria should pay on the considerable trade debt not covered under the insurance schemes of official OECD government export credit agencies (in excess of $4 billion); but progress was being made. Nigeria had originally wanted to complete this refinancing agreement by the end of February, but the talks had been interrupted by the coup. Given the degree of corruption associated with the preceding regime, major questions were being raised about whether some of the goods that were claimed to have been exported to Nigeria ever arrived in the country. Hence, the exact size of the uninsured trade debt became a chief issue. The Nigerian government appointed Chase Manhattan Bank of New York to reconcile claims for trade payments outstanding.

At about the same time, Barclay's Bank of London took the lead in a syndicated loan to Nigeria (of approximately $1 billion) to repay exporters insured by Britain's Export Credits Guarantee Department (ECGD). Barclay's had acted as agent during the July and September 1983 refinancing negotiations and had now been designated to manage a new loan to repay insured exporters. Nigeria's punctual repayment of the first installment on those agreements only a few days after the coup facilitated the reopening of lines of credit.

However, despite the progress in refinancing its $6-to-$7 billion dollar officially insured short-term trade debt, agreement on the balance of Nigeria's $20 billion debt was dependent upon the state of its negotiations with the IMF. A Nigerian team left for Washington on 15 February 1984 to resume discussions with the Fund.

The IMF continued to insist on a major devaluation for the naira. Fund staff and their counterparts in the World Bank agreed that the overvaluation of the naira was the single most important source of economic distortion in Nigeria. In their view, Nigeria had become one of the most extreme cases of overvalued exchange rates and economic distortion in the developing world. The Fund asked for a further review of domestic interest rates and a number of trade policy reforms, including a relaxation of import restrictions, vigorous export promotion, and a simplification and rationalization of Nigeria's tariff structure.

Most of these terms were initially deemed acceptable by Nigeria's finance minister, Onaolapo Soleye. However, the same three issues that had prevented an agreement under the civilians prevented an agreement under the military: devaluation, relaxation of import controls, and the cutting of petroleum subsidies.

DISCUSSION QUESTIONS

1. *Given that Nigeria was making headway in its balance of payments, should the Fund have been so rigid in regard to its conditions? What does this say about how the Fund views balance of payments? Should the Fund have been more flexible in its insistence on the devaluation of the naira?*
2. *When negotiating with a country, should the Fund broaden its conditions to include political objectives, such as human rights, freedom of association and speech, or the security of citizens from arbitrary arrest and imprisonment?*
3. *How do political objectives of governance differ from the ones discussed in the previous section?*
4. *With the World Bank backing the policy recommendation of the Fund, who had the responsibility for taking a broader view of Nigeria's development and of how the Fund's recommendation effected Nigeria's future?*

A DIFFERENCE OF OPINION

The Buhari government did not rule out a devaluation altogether. In fact, it oversaw a gradual reduction in the value of the currency (from 1 naira = $1.38 in 1983 to 1 naira = $1.12 in 1985). But it disagreed strongly on the pace and magnitude of the devaluation requested by the Fund. Nigeria wanted a gradual reduction of approximately 30 percent to bring the naira to parity with the U.S. dollar. The IMF was holding out for a single, more significant cut in Nigeria's exchange rate. Many of the arguments against devaluation that had been employed by the civilian negotiators were used again by the military ones. They continued to argue that because Nigeria's major export, oil, was denominated in dollars, a major devaluation would have no appreciable impact on exports. Furthermore, because Nigerian manufacturers could scarcely provide 50 percent of Nigeria's consumption needs, high levels of imports would have to be maintained. Nigeria's existing industries also relied heavily on imported raw materials and intermediate goods for their production. Finally, the negotiators expressed fear that inflation would rise dramatically in the wake of a major devaluation. Thus, as General Buhari stated in an interview, "devaluation could be considered only as a last resort."

Talks with the Fund continued intermittently throughout spring 1984, as Nigeria's foreign exchange reserves dipped to below the $1 billion level. In early April, a consortium of foreign suppliers, concerned that they might never be repaid, decided to drop their insistence that Nigeria reach an agreement with the Fund and agreed to a rescheduling of its uninsured trade arrears, along the lines of a Nigerian proposal that provided for a two-and-a-half-year grace period and an interest rate of 1 percent above the London Inter-Bank Rate (LIBOR). About $2.5 billion of debts were settled with this agreement.

Talks with the Fund resumed in May 1984, but, fueled by fears of inflation, public resistance to a devaluation began to grow. As the dollar appreciated in its relationship to other major currencies throughout the spring, the naira-dollar relationship remained basically unchanged. Thus, the naira was being revalued upward in relationship to the currencies of its major European trading partners. In June, another Nigerian delegation flew to Washington to explain the country's adjustment package. However, the talks were soon broken off over Nigeria's refusal to agree to a one-time devaluation of 30-35 percent, a reduction of its petroleum subsidies, and a further relaxation of its curbs on imports. In July, the Fund declared that Nigeria's latest proposals for stabilization and adjustment were insufficient for it to qualify for a loan under the Fund's Extended Fund Facility (EFF). The Nigerians had hoped that their austerity program and policy changes would serve as an alternative to a major devaluation, but the Fund rejected their position.

It was at this time that the Buhari government devised a strategy for stabilization without the Fund. Several elements of its approach had been introduced under the guise of austerity shortly after it came to power (e.g., restriction of both imports and demand, emplacement of tight controls on government spending, and an increase of the domestic sources of government finance). The Buhari government had also devised a number of schemes to increase foreign exchange earnings (beginning with appeals to OPEC for an increase in its production quota and continuing with experiments in countertrading, oil price cuts, and deliberate overproduction). However, austerity and increased foreign exchange earnings alone were not enough to cover the interest payments Nigeria had to maintain on its $20 billion debt. After the talks with the IMF broke down in July, Nigeria tried to bypass the Fund and negotiate directly with its principal creditors.

DISCUSSION QUESTIONS

1. *Did the divisions among the creditors to Nigeria prove the moral skeptic to be correct that self-interest is the primary factor guiding international relations?*

2. *The purpose of the Fund's conditions is to allow the servicing and restructuring of a country's foreign debt while the balance of payments is brought into line so as to restore the country's credit rating, attract new funds, and to establish a basis for growth. In some countries in which the Fund's*

conditions have been implemented, rioting and the overthrow of governments have taken place. Should the Fund have been more sensitive to the political situation in Nigeria?

GOING IT ALONE

Buoyed by its recent success in refinancing some of its short-term debt into longer-term maturities, the Buhari government offered to convert its official debt denominated in local currency into promissory notes along the lines agreed to in its April 1984 settlement with uninsured creditors. It bypassed the Paris Club and gave OECD trading agencies until the end of September to reply to the proposal. Britain's ECGD assumed a key role for the creditors and advised its policyholders to insist on an agreement with the IMF and to reject the Nigerian offer. However, there was a rush of creditors (who were owed a total of $2.4 billion) anxious to accept the offer, and Nigeria was more than willing to test the authority of the official agencies (such as Britain's ECGD) that were attempting to control the negotiations. The conversion of local currency principal proved to be more complicated than originally anticipated, however, and the creditors represented at the Paris Club played down the prospects of an agreement without prior Fund approval.

The OECD agencies eventually reasserted their authority to negotiate for officially insured creditors, and, in October, the Paris Club formally rejected Nigeria's proposal. It claimed that 1 percent over LIBOR was inadequate and insisted that any settlement had to await an agreement with the Fund. Nigeria tried to leave the door open for a Paris Club settlement without the Fund agreement and proposed to pay holders of insured debts around $220 million in interest due on obligations from 1983 to 1984. But, for the moment, its attempt to bypass the Fund and the Paris Club had failed.

Informal talks with the IMF resumed briefly at the annual IMF-World Bank meetings in September 1984, but there was little progress made. After the Paris Club rejection in October, the U.S. government stepped up pressure on Nigeria to settle with the Fund, and there were reports of disagreement within the Buhari administration about how to proceed. In November, the IMF staff hinted that it might relax its demands on petroleum subsidies and trade liberalization, *if* Nigeria agreed to a major devaluation. But the talks bogged down in December over the nature of the devaluation necessary for an agreement.

In January 1985, General Buhari set his priorities for the coming year in his annual budget speech. He stressed the need for continued austerity and a nationwide freeze on wages. He indicated that 44 percent of the anticipated foreign exchange earnings of the country were going to be set aside for debt servicing during 1985, giving the country one of the highest debt/service ratios in the world. An IMF team arrived in Lagos for routine discussions later in January and argued for an immediate devaluation of at least 25 percent, followed by a further downward float of another 25 percent. But in an interview after the negotiations in February, Buhari once again reflected such a large devaluation and contended that the devaluation of the naira "is the most sensitive issue as far as we are concerned." He also rejected any reduction in the level of subsidies on domestic fuel.

After only a year in office, Buhari had imposed a severe deflationary stabilization program on the country, without receiving any of the benefits of IMF financial assistance. Public expenditures had been reduced (with severe implications for employment and local business), and strict import licensing had been utilized to cut import levels back to their lowest levels (in current terms) in ten years. At the same time, oil production levels had recovered, the country's negative trade balance had been reversed, foreign exchange reserves were slowly being built up, and new external borrowing had virtually ceased.

Many difficult policy reforms had also been initiated (reduction of the state's role in production, increases in interest rates, and the initiation of a reform in the tax structure). As a result of these policy reforms and the deflationary measures associated with them, thousands of civil servants were laid off, urban unemployment skyrocketed, new taxes were introduced, industrial sector activity was drastically curtailed, and the cost of many social services was passed on to consumers for the first time. Throughout the period, Nigeria continued to pay interest on the portion of its debts that had been rescheduled. In 1984 alone, it paid out $3.5 billion in debt servicing, or 34.2 percent of its total export earnings for the year. In February 1985, Buhari publicly declared his opposition to a 50 to 60 percent devaluation of the naira, and the talks with the IMF were effectively stalled. On 27 August, his government was overthrown by a military coup.

DISCUSSION QUESTIONS

1. *As seen in this case study, commercial banks, private investors, and bilateral donors increasingly looked for an agreement between Nigeria and the Fund before committing their own funds to the country. Is this a form of cooperative coercion on the part of creditors?*
2. *Should the IMF, which is directed toward short-term adjustment programs, be addressing Nigeria's economic problems?*
3. *Should the Fund control the "spigot" through which virtually all other financial loans pass into a developing country such as Nigeria?*

4. *Does the international financial system either inadvertently or intentionally discriminate against developing countries such as Nigeria?*
5. *Given all the measures the Buhari government took toward solvency, should the Fund have given legitimacy to the government by not insisting on a one-time devaluation of the naira?*

FROM STABILIZATION TO ADJUSTMENT

When Major General Ibrahim Babangida assumed power in August 1985, he inherited a stabilized but drastically deflated economy. The external economic conditions confronting the new military government were the worst faced by any regime since independence. Less than four months after it assumed power, the international price for oil fell precipitously. Nigeria's oil income was cut nearly in half. The spot price for Nigerian Bonny Light crude petroleum dropped from $27.88 per barrel in August 1985 to a low of $9.94 in July 1986. The country's debt/service ratio climbed to nearly 40 percent. The foreign exchange reserves that had been built up under Buhari were sufficient to cover import needs, but there was nothing left to draw down. The country had already gone through two years of austerity and economic stagnation, and, with the drop in oil income, the prospects for the short- and medium-terms were grim.

Like the Buhari government that preceded it, the new regime initially established its legitimacy by deliberately correcting the most evident flaws of its predecessor. The new government repealed the controversial Decree No. 4, released those detained without being charged or tried, and announced plans for a restructuring of the powerful national security organization, the NSO. The new leadership was creative, charismatic, and far less insulated and remote than its predecessor. Although northerners continued to dominate the military regime, the Babangida government was not controlled by the same group from the upper north that had played such a prominent role in the Buhari government. Officers from the middle north occupied many of the key military positions in the new regime and were generally much more comfortable than their predecessors in dealing with southern political and economic elites.[5]

Babangida worked populist themes into his early addresses to the nation and demonstrated his originality and independence by being the first of Nigeria's six military leaders to assume the title of "President".[6] He also made a number of bold and highly visible appointments to his cabinet, selecting a unusually large number of professionals who collectively expressed a broad range of views and perspectives—from the populist Ransome-Kuti in Health and the outspoken nationalist Akinyemi in Foreign Affairs to the economic conservative Kalu in Finance. The appointment of Kalu was significant by virtue of the fact that he had formerly been an employee of the World Bank and was widely know as a supporter of accommodation with the IMF.

In his first public statement after the coup, Babangida declared his intention to "break the deadlock" and reopen the stalemated talks with the Fund. For the first time, high-ranking government officials appeared willing to support some of the economic arguments of the Fund. Brigadier Sani Sami stated that he thought it was in Nigeria's best interests to obtain an IMF loan quickly. He urged the Nigerian Economic Society to discuss the issues and consider the possibility of a dual exchange rate. The chair of Nigeria's largest bank, First Bank of Nigeria, also went on record urging a faster depreciation of the naira. Within a few weeks, two committees were set up to look into the major financial issues facing the country. One focused on the IMF terms, and the other concentrated on the costs and benefits of countertrade. It was at this time that the government decided to stimulate informed discussion on the merits of an agreement with the Fund and launched its celebrated national public debate on the issue.

At the outset, it appeared that the government was already predisposed toward some kind of agreement with the Fund and that the public debate was simply a way of generating and mobilizing public support for the tough conditions that would follow.[7] Some observers outside Nigeria (including the IMF) were concerned about the wisdom of opening public discussions on the technical issues of international finance and worried that the new government might find itself locked into an inflexible position on the issue.

The debate itself consisted of a flurry of public speeches, individual pronouncements, street demonstrations, public affairs discussions, and special reports and interviews in newspapers, and on radio and television. It provided a unique glimpse into the composition of the coalitions of supporters and opponents of the agreement with the IMF. At the beginning of the debate, the IMF's demands were published, along with the details of past negotiations. The Fund was still holding out for (1) a substantial devaluation, (2) anti-inflationary measures (such as a reduction in aggregate spending, a tightening of the money supply, a mechanism for increasing the efficiency of parastatals and government investments, and the end of nonstatutory financial transfers to state governments), and (3) the restoration of market mechanisms (e.g., trade liberalization, the removal of petroleum subsidies, cuts in subsidies and loans to parastatals, an increase in interest rates and cuts in credit allocations, and a raising of agricultural producer prices). Privatization was not played up as an issue at this point in the negotiations, but it was evident that the Fund wanted some movement in this direction, along with a review of industrial incentives, an export drive, general improvements in the efficiency of revenue collection, and stricter control and management of Nigeria's external debt.

It did not take long for a broad-based opposition to the Fund's program to emerge. Organized labor declared the program (and the Babangida government) "anti-worker" and contended that the rich would benefit at the expense of the poor. Labor was concerned about the extent of retrenchment already suffered and likely to continue with the IMF program. The Nigerian Labor Congress (NLC) was especially opposed to privatization and called for greater indigenously based industrialization. Labor was joined by a number of urban-based professionals who expressed concern about the disruptive implications of a major devaluation. Many professionals had already been badly hit by nearly two years of economic stagnation under the Buhari regime and were concerned about the implications of extended austerity under the Fund.

Students, academics, and a number of journalists also joined in the coalition opposed to agreement with the Fund. Many expressed concerns that an authoritarian regime would be required to implement the program, and several argued that the debate itself was a thinly disguised corporatist effort to reconstruct the principal factions of the dominant classes, in disarray since the overt repression of the Buhari government.[8] A few beneficiaries of the import-licensing scheme spoke out against trade liberalization, as did a number of prominent northerners who were especially concerned that greater reliance on market mechanisms would disrupt the fragile regional balance in the country. By October, there were reports of disputes within the ruling military council on the wisdom of reaching an agreement with the Fund.

Support for an agreement with the Fund came primarily from prominent indigenous entrepreneurs in the Lagos area, a number of professional economists, the Lagos Chamber of Commerce, and major industrialists (who spoke through the Manufacturer's Association of Nigeria). The World Bank also began to play a larger role in the process at this point. The Bank had been involved in the background of the two-and-a-half-years of discussions with the IMF by virtue of the fact that every IMF mission to Lagos used the Bank's offices and relied on its files of economic data and information about Nigerian officials and policies. The Bank, however, now began to play a much more visibly active role during the public debate. The resident World Bank representative in Nigeria was a Pakistani by the name of Ishrat Hussain. Hussain attended every seminar on the Nigerian economy and took every opportunity to make his (and the Bank's) views known. He was a frequent and occasionally outspoken participant during the public debate on the IMF, and he regularly courted and held receptions for the leading economic elite in the country. According to one of his staff members in the Lagos office, "eventually many of his arguments were espoused by [that elite]."

Nevertheless, there were a few reservations about an IMF agreement within the Nigerian business community, especially among the industrialists. Much as they wanted to see a settlement of the debt issue and a resumption of normal trade for their import-intensive facilities, they were concerned that too much trade liberalization would make their investment inviable. Hence, they favored agreement with the Fund, on the condition that it be accompanied by a major tariff reform.

However eloquent or well-argued their case, supporters of an agreement were drowned out by the majority opposed to the Fund. Public opinion grew increasingly hostile throughout the fall, and, once again, the same three issues that bedeviled previous attempts to reach an agreement emerged as major stumbling blocks: devaluation, trade liberalization, and an end to petroleum subsidies. But the public debate also revealed a new issue. It became increasingly apparent that there was a growing reticence on the part of the public about any further government borrowing from *any* source. That is, more than opposition to borrowing from the IMF, there was widespread opposition to the idea of additional government borrowing in general. After years of seeing one corrupt government after another, Nigerians had become fed up and were increasingly suspicious of the ability of its leaders to manage the economy properly. Many argued that if more loans were obtained, the money would disappear just as quickly as it had in the past.

In the wake of growing public discontent, major strikes planned by both the NLC and students' organizations, and further disputes within the ruling military council, Nigeria broke off talks with the IMF on 13 December 1985. Babangida's attempt to use the public debate to build a coalition on behalf of an agreement with the Fund had clearly failed.

However, a few weeks later, in his annual budget speech delivered on 31 December 1985, President Babangida combined nationalist assertiveness with an acceptance of most the IMF's original terms—including two of the three issues that had prevented agreement in the past. The nationalist assertiveness was contained in Babangida's call for a reduction in external dependence, for the achievement of food self-sufficiency, for a shift in Nigerian attitudes and tastes, and for a 30 percent cap on debt servicing for the year. But the most significant parts of the speech laid out the plans for major structural adjustments of the economy. According to one IMF official, "The IMF read the budget speech with surprise. The nature of the language was good. We had no idea of what it would mean in policy terms."

Babangida had apparently accepted the public verdict on the IMF but argued that because Nigerians were not willing to borrow additional resources from the Fund, they would have to be prepared to accept tough new economic measures at home. Accordingly, he announced plans for the adoption of a "realistic exchange rate" (one which would allow the naira to find its own level), a substantial (80 percent) reduction of petroleum subsidies, and a large-scale privatization program (an idea traditionally promoted more within the World Bank than the IMF). Explicit reference to trade liberalization was omitted for the time being, but all of the other major components of the Fund's original terms found their way into the speech.

Despite Babangida's rejection of the prevailing public sentiment on the details of the IMF's terms, initial reactions to his speech were generally favorable within Nigeria. The nationalist rhetoric was well received by the Nigerian public. Babangida's references to the most controversial of the Fund's conditions (devaluation and privatization) were vague, especially because the effective consequence of creating a two-tier foreign exchange regime (i.e., a major devaluation) was not evident to the vast majority. Two weeks after his annual budget speech, Babangida announced the formation of a seventeen-member political bureau with the mandate to design a more viable political and economic structure for the country and to lay the groundwork for a return to civilian rule. The Political Bureau was also asked to analyze the contributions made in the national debate on the IMF.

Reaction abroad was guarded. For its part, the IMF expressed doubts about the ability of the Nigerian government (however well-intentioned) to implement its austerity program. And on an official visit to London in early January, the Nigerian foreign minister received a cool reception, allegedly because of rumors of an endorsement of Nigeria's new limit on debt servicing. Nevertheless, there were rumors of an endorsement of Nigeria's new economic recovery program from some significant parties abroad, most notably within the United Kingdom's Export Credit Guarantee Department.

DISCUSSION QUESTIONS

1. *How did the Babangida government seek to preserve its political legitimacy?*
2. *What was the purpose of having a public national discussion on the merits of signing an agreement with the Fund?*
3. *What were the distributive effects of Babangida's proposal? Should his government have taken other steps to further protect certain groups?*

THE STRUCTURAL ADJUSTMENT PROGRAM

Throughout the first half of 1986, work went forward on the development of the two-tier foreign exchange market mechanism and other details of the new economic recovery program. In April, a ninety-day moratorium on repayments of medium- and long-term commercial bank debt was agreed to in London. Nigeria's principal commercial bank creditors agreed to a moratorium on approximately $7.5 billion of its debts. Nigeria also went to the Paris Club in April, but it was unable to secure a comparable moratorium on outstanding debt without some kind of settlement with the Fund. Later that month, Ernest Stern, a senior World Bank vice president, visited Nigeria and declared its program essentially "sound." Stern's endorsement was significant because he was one of the most powerful individuals within the Bank and was widely known as the Bank's "hands-on man" in charge of operations.

In June 1986, President Babangida announced a new two-year structural adjustment program (SAP), which spelled out the details of the plan first introduced in general terms in his budget speech the previous December. The details of the second-tier foreign exchange market (popularly known as SFEM) that served as the cornerstone for the program had been the subject of extensive negotiations between the Bank, the Fund, and the Nigerian government for some time. The Nigerians had originally preferred a small market, secondary to the official market that would continue to handle all government transactions. The World Bank wanted a SFEM of at least $2 billion (large enough to absorb funds that would otherwise go to the black market). The IMF held out for a market that would be large enough to handle all international transactions (including government imports) and one that could absorb the entire official market within a period of six months. The details of the SFEM announced by Babangida were closest to the proposal put forward by the World Bank, and it was increasingly apparent that the Bank was playing a major role in the design of Nigeria's adjustment program. All transactions were to be handled by the SFEM, with the exception of government debt service payments and contributions to international organizations and institutions. The SFEM was to commence on 1 October and coexist with the official market for a period of twelve to fifteen months before being completely absorbed.

The two-tier foreign exchange market was to be accompanied by extensive trade liberalizations and a major privatization program. Nigeria's system of bureaucratic controls was to be dismantled, along with its controversial import-licensing scheme. Six of its major agricultural commodity boards were abolished, and a review of the parastatal sector was initiated. The IMF, however, remained doubtful about the ability of Nigeria to implement its program, declared its dislike of the SFEM program, and continued to hold out for a major devaluation of the naira. The Fund was increasingly "positive" toward Nigeria, but a formal agreement (one that could have provide $1.5 billion from the IMF and up to $1 billion from the Bank) remained elusive. After the announcement of the SAP, however, the World Bank offered to provide $400 million in structural adjustment loans to Nigeria. The commercial bank moratorium originally announced in April 1986 was extended for an additional three months in June.

A week after the announcement of the SAP, the government advanced the SFEM start-up date to 1 August, and the Central Bank issued operational guidelines that significantly relaxed the existing exchange control regulations. A number of interest groups and businesses pressured the Central Bank to allow them to continue operating at the official exchange rate, but the Central Bank agreed only to exempt transactions already in process. In effect, the major consequence of this action was to postpone for three months the full impact of the introduction of the second-tier foreign exchange market.

In early September, shortly before the first SFEM auction, the World Bank announced agreement on a $450 million trade promotion and export development loan (largely to help start and finance the SFEM) and also promised to increase its project lending to Nigeria to nearly $1 billion a year. The London Club agreed to yet another ninety-day extension of Nigeria's debt service moratorium, but was unable to reach a broader agreement due to cross-conditionalities on Nigeria's accumulated debt. The London Club is the forum within which debtor countries negotiate the restructuring of private sector debt with their main creditor banks. Accordingly, on 19 September, Nigeria requested IMF endorsement of its structural adjustment program in the form of a standard standby agreement that would allow Nigeria to borrow, in principle, funds totaling $785 million for an initial period ending in December 1987.

When the first second-tier foreign exchange auction was held on 26 September 1986, the naira fell 68.6 percent to a level of 4.62 naira to the dollar. At the second auction a week later, the naira dropped another 9.2 percent and reached the level of 5.08 to the dollar. After some erratic fluctuations throughout the fall (and a fair degree of Central Bank intervention), the rate stabilized at about 3.5 naira to the dollar, or an effective devaluation of about 57 percent.

In the middle of November 1986, after a month and a half of experience with SFEM, the IMF declared Nigeria eligible for a $540 million standby loan. The Nigerian government refused the funds, but the long-standing deadlock over the rescheduling of Nigeria's $20 to $22 billion of external debts was finally broken. Within weeks of the November agreement with the IMF, the London Club provisionally agreed on a rescheduling plan, and the Paris Club followed with an agreement in the middle of December. All that remained was the formidable task of keeping the agreements on track.

DISCUSSION QUESTIONS

1. *By working behind the scenes and backing up the IMF, did the World Bank engage in unethical collusion?*

2. *Do existing inequalities in international wealth and power act as constraints on efforts of developing countries such as Nigeria to overcome poverty and dependency?*
3. *According to the cosmopolitan, did the IMF engage in just practices and promote just policies? Why or why not?*
4. *Does the economic model endorsed by the IMF and the World Bank blind these institutions to other sets of policies that might have produced a better outcome for Nigeria?*
5. *A country such as Nigeria, which exports a limited range of products with a not very promising long-term growth prospect, has little alternative but to continue to expand its exports. But with the expansion of export goods, there will be a further deterioration in its terms of trade, leading to continued transfer of funds from Nigeria, a poor country, to the world's rich. Should the Fund concern itself with the ethical implications of the distribution patterns its policies promote? Which institutions should address the justness of the distribution of resources with global patterns of transfer of funds and trade? If not the Fund, then who?*

NOTES

1. The north is the least-developed region of the country and has long feared and opposed southern economic penetration. Historically, northern technocrats and intellectuals have favored a strong state role in the economy to counteract the competitive superiority of the southern bourgeoisie. Thomas Biersteker, *Multinationals, the State and Control of the Nigerian Economy* (Princeton, N.J.: Princeton University Press, 1987), pp. 160-161.

2. Larry Diamond, "Nigeria in Search of Democracy," *Foreign Affairs* 62, no. 4 (Spring 1983) 905-927.

3. Larry Diamond, "Nigeria Between Dictatorship and Democracy," *Current History* (May 1987): 201-224.

4. Yusaf Bangura, "Structural Adjustment and the Political Question," *Review of African Political Economy*, no. 37, (December 1986): 24-38, especially pp. 30-31.

5. Information was provided to Thomas Biersteker during a personal communication with Larry Diamond.

6. Larry Diamond, "Nigeria Between Dictatorship and Democracy," *Current History* (May 1987): 201-204.

7. Yusaf Bangura, "Structural Adjustment," p. 32.

8. *Ibid.*

FURTHER READING ON NIGERIA AND THE IMF

Books

Biersteker, Thomas J. *Multinationals, the State and Control of the Nigerian Economy.* Princeton, N.J.: Princeton University Press, 1987.

Gwin, Catherine, Richard Feinberg, and contributors. *Pulling Together: The International Monetary Fund in a Multipolar World.* New Brunswick, N.J.: Transaction Books, 1989.

Myers, Robert J., ed. *The Political Morality of the International Monetary Fund.* Ethics and Foreign Policy Series, vol. 3 New Brunswick, N.J.: Transaction Books, 1987.

Nelson, Joan M., et al., eds. *Fragile Coalitions: The Politics of Economic Adjustment.* New Brunswick, N.J.: Transaction Books, 1989.

Articles

Abdul Raheem, Tajudeen et al., "Editorial: Nigeria: Oil, Debts, and Democracy," *Review of African Political Economy,* no. 37, (December 1986): 6-10.

Bangura, Yusaf, "Structural Adjustment and the Political Question," *Review of African Political Economy,* no. 37, (December 1986): 24-38.

Diamond, Larry, "Nigeria in Search of Democracy," *Foreign Affairs* 62, no. 4 (Spring 1983): 905-927.

Diamond, Larry, "Nigeria Between Dictatorship and Democracy," *Current History* (May 1987): 201-204.

Forrest, Tom, "The Political Economy of Civil Rule and the Economic Crisis in Nigeria (1979-84)," *Review of African Political Economy,* no. 35 (May 1986): 4-26.

Olukoshi, Adebayo and Tajudeen Abdul Raheem, "Nigeria, Crisis Management Under the Buhari Administration," *Review of African Political Economy,* no. 34, (December 1985): 95-101.

6

GATT FAIR TRADE PRACTICES: EUROPEAN COMMUNITY ENLARGEMENT AND THE UNITED STATES

The Nigeria case examined the cardinal role the IMF plays between debtor nations and international creditors. This case, however, looks at the ineffectiveness of an existing international regime, the General Agreement on Tariffs and Trade, or GATT, to resolve a dispute between two members. Issues of distributive justice arise in this case. What constitutes adequate compensation, and what are fair procedures for resolving disputes between GATT members involving on trade practices? This case study shows how ultimately international cooperation and compromise are needed to protect domestic agricultural markets.

In 1986, the European Community (EC) incorporated Spain and Portugal as members. As a result, the United States experienced a sharp increase in trade barriers to its feed grain exports. Representatives from the EC in Brussels acknowledged that the United States was entitled to compensation for the harm done to its balance of payments. But, the EC pointed out, it was predicted that in the long run the enlargement would increase U.S.

This chapter is an edited version of the case study by John Odell and Margit Matzinger-Tchakerian, "European Community Enlargement and the United States," Pew case study no. 130.

exports of industrial goods to the EC, providing adequate compensation overall. Washington rejected such an interpretation of the GATT rules. The United States argued that the GATT rules required compensation to be made to the sector being harmed. Because U.S. farmers were being harmed by the change in tariffs, it was they who should be compensated.

The GATT rules on compensation were sufficiently ambiguous as to be unhelpful in resolving the dispute between the EC and the United States. Furthermore, both parties refused to acknowledge the GATT commission's authority in mediating a resolution. Due to their relatively equal bargaining positions, the EC and the United States were able to reach a mutually acceptable resolution. As GATT members what responsibility do the United States and the EC have to abide by its rules? Is it inevitable that national trade agendas will take precedence over mutual international issues such as global economic stability? If GATT is ineffective, is there some notion of fairness that most countries voluntarily play by? And if not, what entity will determine what are fair trade practices?

* * *

In late 1985, after seven years of complex and difficult negotiations, the European Community of Ten (EC-10) reached agreement with Spain and Portugal to integrate them as new members of the EC. Almost immediately in 1986, however, enlargement touched off a surprising, major commercial dispute between the EC of Twelve (EC-12) and the United States.

INTERESTS IN CONFLICT

The treaties of accession, to take formal effect on 1 March 1986, would mean, among other things, changes in Spanish and Portuguese tariff systems so as to bring them in line with the common EC external tariff. During a ten-year transition period, duties on manufactured imports to Spain and Portugal would decline from an average of 15 percent to the EC level of 5 percent, and the two governments would also have to relax quantitative restrictions.

At the same time, however, their barriers to certain agricultural products would rise sharply as they came under the EC Common Agricultural Policy (CAP). Spanish tariffs on imported feed grains, now at 20 percent, would soon exceed 100 percent. In addition, the treaty guaranteed 15 percent of Portugal's grain import market to its new European partners, and it established a new quota limiting soybean and soybean oil imports for domestic human consumption. Both of the Portugal measures would expire after a transitional period, during which the new member would adjust its national programs toward the EC system.

Most observers acknowledged that, among other things, this latest EC enlargement would destroy substantial current U.S. farm exports to the Iberian countries. Early statements from the U.S. side charged that the annual U.S. loss in sales could be as much as $1 billion. Both Spain and Portugal had deficits in feed-grain supplies and relied on imports in the early 1980s, and U.S. farmers were by far the dominant foreign suppliers in both countries. The bulk of the trade at issue as a result of the EC enlargement was corn (maize). Soybeans are also a major U.S. export item. Feed grains are used by livestock producers as feed for hogs, chickens, and cattle. (Table 6.1 gives definitions of relevant commodity categories.)

Washington had long held that GATT's international rules permit customs unions only if the required tariff changes make third parties no worse off in any product category. The United States would thus be entitled to compensation if any state, in order to join such a union, withdrew a product concession granted to the United States in a previous negotiation. In 1967, Spain had bound its import tariffs on corn and sorghum at an upper limit of 20 percent in return for similar concessions from Washington, and EC enlargement meant unbinding (in order to raise) Spanish tariffs on cereals. Portugal had not bound these tariffs. Washington had two other complaints concerning Portugal. The United States flatly branded the 15 percent grain quote reserved for the EC-10 as illegal, according to its understanding of the GATT, and it also objected strenuously to the soybean restriction.

The European Community's equally long-standing legal position held that the GATT requires parties forming a customs union to compensate third parties only if those nations' interests are damaged on the whole, not on a product-by-product basis. EC "debits" on cereals would be offset by any "credits earned" by third countries on other products. Spanish and Portuguese industrial protection was quite high, and Brussels showed that after accession was completed, the average level of protection—combining industrial and agricultural sectors—would clearly be lower in both countries, not higher. The United States was getting more than enough compensation for feed grains already, via other products, and thus was not entitled to more.

U.S. officials questioned whether the United States would benefit from the decrease in Spanish and Portuguese industrial tariffs. Iberian tariffs on manufactures from West Germany and other EC countries would go all the way to zero, giving them preferential access that would be difficult for American factories to overcome.

American Farm Crisis

For U.S. farmers, the stakes seemed large. Spain and Portugal had been the third most important export markets for U.S. feed grains. In 1982,

TABLE 6.1 Selected Commodity Classifications

Grains and feeds
  -feed grains
    barley
    corn
    grain sorghums
    oats, rye
  -feed grain products
  -feeds and fodders
    corn by-products (gluten)
    alfalfa meal and cubes
    citrus pellets
    other
  -wheat
  -wheat flour
  -bulgur wheat
  -rice
  -blended food products
  -other grain

Oilseeds and products
  -oilseeds
    soybeans
    sunflower seeds
    other seeds
  -oilcake and meal
    soybean meal
    other
  -protein substances
  -vegetable oil

Source: John Odell and Margit Matzinger-Tchakerian, *European Community Enlargement and the United States*, Pew case study no. 130, Annex 1 (Philadelphia, Pa.: The Pew Charitable Trusts, 1988), p. 22.

together they had bought 15 percent of U.S. exports, mostly of corn and sorghum, a figure that had declined to less than 8 percent by 1985. In early 1986, the U.S. government estimated the value of sales to be lost to Spain at around $640 million per year. The estimate for annual lost sales to Portugal was put at about $55 million. U.S. grain farmers demanded that the EC compensate them fully for these losses. They further insisted that the new EC variable duties should not be imposed until such compensation had been made. The argument that the United States benefited from the lowering of industrial trade barriers did not impress U.S. farmers at all. For them, compensation to American sectors other than grains was unacceptable. After all, as one farmer put it, "We are the ones with our dollars on the line."[1]

U.S. agricultural markets in Spain and Portugal seemed all the more crucial in the context of the general depression of farm exports and incomes. During the 1970s and early 1980s, U.S. farmers had responded to an increase in world demand by buying more land and boosting production. World food shortages, rapid growth in world population and in the income of foreign markets, in combination with a weak U.S. dollar, had sent agricultural exports sky-high.

By the mid-1980s, however, some of the importing countries had attained self-sufficiency, and others had been hit by the debt crisis. The soaring dollar exchange rate had made all U.S. products more costly relative to competing supplies. U.S. farm exports dropped sharply, from a record peak of $44 billion in 1981 to what was to be a ten-year low of under $27 billion in 1986. Shrinking export possibilities pushed U.S. agriculture and related sectors into a dramatic slump. Some areas were haunted by an epidemic of farm foreclosures and large-scale unemployment. "Farmers and agribusiness can't survive much longer than [this year]," Senator John Melcher (D-Mont.) told Secretary of Agriculture Richard Lyng in July 1986.[2] Newspapers of the time were filled with stories of despondent farmers committing suicide. No national politician could afford to appear insensitive to this plight.

In the eyes of U.S. farmers, their malaise was not entirely due to adverse market conditions. They especially blamed the unfair trade practices of the EC, which had been laid down in the CAP. Since its imposition in the early 1960s, the CAP has been to U.S. farmers what a red flag is to a bull. Washington challenged the CAP from the start, thereby triggering the "chicken war" of 1962-1963. In this dispute, the United States protested an EC tariff on poultry imports that had been imposed as a result of CAP regulation. The United States claimed that the poultry tariff and the concomitant CAP regulation were illegal under GATT and therefore should be eliminated. Brussels refused to offer compensation, and the United States imposed retaliatory tariffs after a GATT panel fixed the amount at $26 million worth of trade. The United States failed to make a fundamental dent in the CAP.

The EC had expanded twice previously, and each occasion had left a bad taste in American farmers' mouths. "U.S. farmers have been stung twice before when countries have acceded to the EC without adequate compensation," one U.S. trade official told reporters, "and Washington does not intend to stand by and let it happen again."[3] Senator Pete Wilson

(R-Calif.) echoed the same concerns when he charged that no compensation was offered to the United States during the 1973 and 1981 enlargements. "Unless we defend our farmers from the beginning they will never get the compensation the European Community owes them."[4]

Americans, especially California orange and lemon growers, had complained since 1976 about EC arrangements granting preferential access for citrus products from Mediterranean countries. In response, in June 1985 Washington slapped the EC with a 40 percent tariff on pasta exports. The EC counterretaliated with higher tariffs on U.S. lemons and walnuts, trade valued at about $30 million. The EC states felt the CAP itself was under attack.[5]

In addition to restricting farm imports to the EC, the CAP affected markets in third countries. High EC internal prices generated surpluses of many commodities, including cereals, which Brussels moved into the world market by means of export subsidies. The EC had changed from a net importer to a net exporter of grains. Americans denounced EC dumping in third markets as one of the chief causes of their loss in export market shares. By the mid-1980s furious U.S. farmers were vowing to fight the subsidy issue to the bitter end. A senior official of the U.S. Department of Agriculture declared in 1986, "for the next few years there is going to be blood on the floor."[6]

DISCUSSION QUESTIONS

1. *How do the EC and the United States each interpret entitlement to compensation according to the GATT international rules? How does the compensation outcome differ according to each interpretation?*

2. *What is a just system of compensation? Should the American farmers who are economically harmed by the changes in trade concessions themselves be compensated? Or, given that U.S. industry stands to benefit from the changes, are the benefits to the U.S. industrial sector just compensation for the losses to U.S. farmers?*

3. *As long as subsidies benefit the members of the EC, on what grounds can the United States claim that the EC subsidies are unfair?*

EUROPEAN COMMON INTERESTS

On the other side of the Atlantic, EC member states had their own strongly held viewpoints on these problems. The EC is a huge player in world trade. EC exports, not including sales between member states, accounted for roughly one-fifth of world trade in 1985.[7]

The EC is also a different player, more than simply a summation of the members' interests. These states share a general interest in preserving their EC institutions and strengthening their influence in the larger world, despite their sometimes conflicting interests in specific commercial issues. Although they often remain under the surface, these common interests reach well beyond the commercial realm. The original European Community was founded in the wake of World War II on the premise that economic interdependence between Germany and France would prevent further bloodshed between the two traditional enemies. The German government's fundamental foreign policy required a strong European coalition in which to anchor itself. Britain, France, and Italy recognized that as only a middle power, they could no longer hope to rival the USSR or the United States in world influence without joining forces. Their greatest opportunities to do so were through the EC on economic issues. Thus each state's inclination to fight for its separate interests was constrained at least to some extent by its need for cooperation on other issues and by the long-term cost of pushing partners all the way to disintegration of the common institution.

It has often been said that the CAP was the fundamental glue that made possible the European Community's original cohesion. France in particular was unwilling to join if such a union did not provide a common market for farm products. France needed the enlarged market for its still substantial agricultural labor force. During the subsequent years and despite other changes, the CAP continued to be the European Community's most heavily guarded policy. An attack on the CAP therefore implicitly challenged the basic common interest in the EC itself. One EC official reiterated during the 1986 dispute with the United States: "The Community is determined that the fundamental objectives and mechanisms, both internal and external, of the common agricultural policy shall not be placed in question."[8]

What, then, are those basic objectives and mechanisms? In summary, the CAP's declared goals are to maintain European food security, stable prices, "fair" prices for consumers, and farm incomes. In practice, though, the last objective has become the overriding policy goal. The central means for maintaining farm income is a set of techniques for supporting official prices. The member states and the EC Commission set a single, Community-wide minimum price for a particular crop, and then if supplies are excessive at that price, the EC Commission purchases the surplus and pays to store it.

Of course unlimited imports of cheaper goods from outside the Community would defeat such a program. Therefore, a second main technique is the variable import levy. When the price of a foreign product is less than the EC price, a levy equivalent to the difference is collected at the frontier, raising the import price to a level slightly higher than goods produced within the EC. Thus, no matter how efficient non-EC producers may be, their goods will never be competitive inside the EC. Understandably, the protective variable levy causes strong resentment among competitors around the world, not only in the United States

Over the years, as European farmers increased their productivity, rising official EC internal prices induced the mushrooming surplus production of several products, even of crops that could never be economic in northern climates without subsidy. Excess EC stocks became an expensive scandal. As one remedy for unwanted stocks, Brussels also disposed of some by subsidizing exports outside the EC. Subsidies are necessary because world prices are often much lower than EC prices. In 1992, partly because of the subsidies, the EC is the world's second largest exporter of agricultural goods, right behind the United States. Finally, the CAP embodied the principle of "Community preference," which stipulated that member states should purchase imports from each other before turning to other countries.

The intervention purchases, stocks, and export subsidies (called "restitutions") became such a heavy burden on the EC budget as to divide the member states and even pose occasional threats of European Community breakdown. Vigorous internal criticism had led to several major European proposals for CAP reform, but far-reaching changes had not been implemented. Mediterranean enlargement added to the burdens because the EC was absorbing new countries whose large agricultural systems were in dire need of improvement.

Of course most other nations, including the United States, have also long operated programs to maintain and if necessary to subsidize farm incomes. GATT rules from the beginning incorporated a huge loophole insulating U.S. and other parties' agricultural sectors from its liberalizing disciplines. The U.S. system also operates via price supports, although with different techniques. The United States imposes barriers to imports of some, though not many, commodities to protect its official prices from less expensive foreign products. In the 1950s when one of these programs was challenged as a violation of U.S. GATT obligations, Washington sought and received a blanket and indefinite waiver of those obligations regarding all of its farm programs. The United States also established its "Food for Peace" program partly as a means of government disposal of surpluses as aid to poorer countries.

In the 1980s the magnitude of government subsidies to U.S. farmers ballooned to enormous size. Overproduction and uncompetitive export prices were piling up surplus stocks in the United States too. The United States generally resisted adopting outright export subsidies for farm goods until the mid-1980s. At that time, Washington began selective subsidized sales, attacking European competitors in third markets. The Americans acknowledged that their own kettle was also black, but indicated readiness to negotiate away their agriculture waiver if the EC and others would agree to discipline their own market-distorting programs.

EC Enlargement, Democracy, and the Maize Market

EC enlargement, like EC origins, was driven by political as well as economic objectives. In fact, French, Italian, German, and other leaders favored the assimilation of Spain and Portugal even at some commercial discomfort to their countries, because they felt membership would reinforce the neighboring former dictatorships' democratic political stability and help prevent them from slipping toward alignment with the East. Considering enlargement from the economic angle, one of Europe's most influential farm leaders explained:

> We are not happy about that. It creates greater farm competition. We would be just as happy to keep them out. But we understand the political reasons. We said the Americans should understand that the political reasons are important to them too. Not as farmers, but as Americans. You have to pay a price for consolidating democracy and avoiding a shift to the left. You can't simply insist on maintaining your same commercial rights.[9]

The EC had long used geopolitical arguments to justify its preferential arrangements with Mediterranean and developing countries, and once the United States had established its preferential Caribbean Basin Initiative (CBI) in the 1980s, Europeans also cited the CBI as a precedent.

One of the particular flash points of farmer opposition to enlargement was fruits and vegetables. French and Italian growers would lose business to efficient competitors in the new Mediterranean member states. In France, it was quite clear that agriculture as a whole tolerated the enlargement package on the understanding that their losses in fruits and vegetables would be offset by a significant gain: expansion of French corn sales in Spain and Portugal.[10] French corn growers expected the market in the two countries to be between 5 and 8 million tons a year.[11] Enlargement would take import demand away from the United States and give it to the France, in keeping with European Community preference.

On the specific maize issue, member states had different interests. France was the largest producer—growing nearly half of the EC-12 crop of 1984-1985—and the only state producing a surplus relative to domestic consumption. Most French corn grows in the southwest region just across the Pyrenees from Spain. Italy was the second largest producer. Spain would be the third. The largest EC importers of grain maize were Spain, the Netherlands, West Germany, and Portugal. Thus one of the European Community's three most powerful states was a maize exporter, and the other two—West Germany and the United Kingdom—were both importers.

Spain had long been a net corn importer, and, during the accession negotiations, its government asked the EC to allow a reduced levy on corn, to permit continued access to those U.S. supplies. Economic trends, however, were changing during the 1980s. In Spain, production was expanding. In both Spain and Portugal imports were falling sharply even before accession. The high value of the dollar made U.S. corn costly. The Spanish government and farmers were attempting to improve irrigation and yields, however. The Spanish corn deficit, the balm for French agriculture's wounds, was already evaporating before the beginning of the U.S. dispute.

Another market trend was also working against corn growers throughout the EC. Yields and supplies were increasing due to technical progress, but the official cereals price was also rising. As a result, livestock producers were shifting from cereals to other animal feeds. European use of corn in animal feed was falling in the 1980s. The major substitutes were manioc, imported from Thailand and Indonesia, and, in some areas, corn gluten feed, which is a by-product of corn processing and a U.S. export. Prior to accession, Spain had prohibited the import of these substitutes; now the Spanish market would be open to these threats to corn.

It might appear that Dutch and German dairy farmers and others who buy feed grain would have an interest in opposing corn growers. The price of feed, however, is held up by the official CAP price, whether the corn comes from Iowa or Bordeaux. If the EC corn supply increases relative to demand, the price does not fall because Brussels buys the surplus, with the entire EC budget bearing the burden. Feeders would like to see lower feed prices, but more fundamentally, they also depend directly on the CAP to support their own output prices. Dairy farmers in particular help produce one of the largest surplus products; thus, splitting agriculture politically is difficult.

European Farm Crisis

Despite the CAP, during the mid-1980s European farmers, including corn growers, were suffering a painful decline in real income similar to their North American counterparts. In 1985, agricultural real income dropped to its lowest point in fifteen years. French cereal growers suffered a 20 percent shrinkage in net revenue that year as costs rose and output prices slid.[12] Urgent pleas for help were mounting on the desks of national parliamentarians and EC officials in Brussels, just as in Washington.

European farmers have traditionally been influential in shaping EC as well as national politics. Agriculture still accounted for some 8 percent of EC employment in 1980, in contrast to about 2 percent in the United States. Farmers in Europe are quite well organized on both national and supranational levels. They coordinate and mobilize their mass support through the Comite des Organisations Professionelles Agricoles des Pays de la Communaute Europeene (COPA). This umbrella organization of national farm federations agrees on a common policy position on behalf of all commodity groups in all states, thus preventing groups from being turned one against the other politically. In France, politicians of all sorts were courting farmers in their effort to gain votes for the March 1986 national elections.

In the national capitals, the member states felt somewhat different interests in international trade in general. The Federal Republic of Germany had a large and rising export surplus, but France, Italy, and the United Kingdom were all experiencing overall deficits. In 1985, the French and the British current accounts improved, but the Italian accounts deteriorated. The economies of France, Italy, and Germany had been growing more slowly than that of the United States and both unemployment and inflation were worse in most of Western Europe than they were in the United States.

The United States and the EC were each the other's most important trading partner. Twenty-one percent of total U.S. exports went to the EC in 1985; and the U.S. share of EC exports to third parties was also 21 percent that year. These EC goods represented only 10 percent of members' exports, including intra-EC trade (see Table 6.2). The stakes involved in the EC enlargement dispute do not seem as large when seen in relation to the total trade flow between the United States and the EC, which exceeded $100 billion going both ways.

DISCUSSION QUESTIONS

1. *Is there an international consensus that free trade is the norm?*
2. *According to what ethical framework could it be said that other countries were taking unfair advantage of the U.S. market?*
3. *Is there something unfair about the EC's protective variable levy? Is there something unjust about guaranteeing the EC farmers a market for their goods? Give reasons.*
4. *Given that the economies of France, Italy, and Germany had been growing at a slower pace than that of the United States and that both unemployment and inflation were worse in most of Western Europe than in the United States, does the cosmopolitan's standard of justice warrant the preferential action taken by the EC?*
5. *The economic stakes involved in the enlargement dispute between the United States and the EC were a significant portion of the total trade taking place between the two entities. If this were not the case, what distributive issue would be at stake?*

TABLE 6.2   United States and EC Trade and Trade Dependence
(value in million U.S. dollars)

Exports to:		*World*	*U.S.*	*EC*
From				
World	1960	127,800	14,740	27,500
	1979	1,537,100	204,720	573,880
	1985	1,783,800	328,211	599,786
U.S.	1960	20,380	----	3,420
	1979	182,025	----	42,654
	1985	213,144	----	45,777
EC	1960	29,730	2,240	10,250
	1979	598,940	36,002	319,766
	1985	649,692	65,388	337,433

Note: EC exports to the world include exports from one member state to another. Data for 1960 apply to the EC-6; 1979 to the EC-9; and 1985 to the EC-10.

Source: 1960 data: *Yearbook of International Trade Statistics* (New York: United Nations, 1963); United Nations, New York. 1979 and 1985 data: *Directory of Trade Statistics* 1986 Yearbook (Washington, D.C.: IMF, 1986).

U.S. OPTIONS, MARCH 1986

In early 1986, when they examined the effect EC enlargement would have on grain exports, Washington leaders were genuinely stunned. The administration's first reaction was to insist on adequate compensation and request a delay in implementation of the enlargement until negotiations could provide that compensation. They also complained that the EC had not provided sufficient information in a timely manner.

The EC rejected both the delay and the accusation. The schedule for implementation had been laid down in a treaty that had been debated for six years and then ratified by twelve national parliaments. EC ambassador to

Washington Roy Denman explained: "There is no, repeat no, requirement in the international trading rules for adjustment by the acceding states of the Customs Union being delayed until agreement has been reached with other trading partners."[13]

The European Community said it had acted in precisely the same way as in earlier enlargements and had kept the Americans fully informed at every stage. A few years later, in fact, one Brussels negotiator recalled that the U.S. position on compensation itself "was something of a shock, almost a complete surprise." Another European official, however, added:

> On paper it was obvious there would be third-party implications of enlargement, but negotiating this took so many years. It took so much stamina, that when agroup of ministers is sitting in a room at 3 o'clock in the morning, and they have just managed to finish negotiating the internal problems, if someone mentions the third-party implications, the natural human response is "to hell with that—we'll take care of it later." In practice these things just don't get taken care of all at once.[14]

Another EC negotiator thought, with hindsight, that "an early EC warning to the United States might have been helpful. They were really shocked."[15] The Americans conceded that they too might have devoted more attention earlier. Although there had been much staff monitoring and computer analysis, the issue had not been a high priority at the policy level.

On 12 February 1986, the GATT in Geneva established a working group to examine the effects of enlargement on the European Community's trading partners. The United States and the EC had previously brought complaints against one another in Geneva, where panels of independent specialists were appointed to render an opinion on the merits and to encourage bilateral settlements. In some cases, the parties reached a resolution before the panel concluded its work; in others, the panel had ruled for one side and the other had implemented the suggestions. But both the EC and the United States had also persuaded a panel to rule in its favor, only to see the other thumb its nose by preventing the GATT Council from formally adopting the panel report. Such experiences had caused a loss of respect for the GATT as an institution for protecting trade interests.

On 3 March, U.S. Trade Representative Clayton Yeutter reportedly telephoned EC Commissioner Willy de Clercq and expressed anger at the EC tariff increases just implemented. The following week de Clercq offered informally to begin discussions of U.S. complaints as soon as possible.[16]

The EC Council asked the Commission to explore possibilities for a negotiated settlement. It reminded the Commission that "the solution should conform to the international trading rules, the principles of the Common

Agricultural Policy and to the enlargement Treaty with Spain and Portugal."[17] Subsequently, EC negotiators approached the United States with the idea of negotiating their dispute under GATT Article XXIV:6. The United States rejected the idea of waiting for lengthy GATT proceedings. U.S. farmers would feel their losses soon and could not afford to wait.

The EC responded to the U.S. complaints about corn and sorghum in Spain by pointing out that Spain already had in place a national tariff that included a variable element, so that the EC system should not significantly change U.S. access to Spain. Both the EC as a whole and Spain would continue to import these grains. Moreover, they said, the United States might be able to increase its sales of such grain substitutes as corn gluten feed. If the EC duty on that product were to be applied in Spain and Portugal, this would mean a significant reduction in existing barriers. Any need for compensation could be determined through negotiations.

Regarding Portugal, the EC explained that the country had formerly controlled its grain imports through a protectionist state monopoly. Lisbon had agreed to dismantle this system gradually, and the 15 percent reservation for EC suppliers would end after a four-year discretionary licensing to help protect its competing olive oil producers. As a part of entry into the EC, Lisbon had agreed to replace this unpredictable soybean licensing system with a more transparent quota system for five years and was to reduce its soybean tariff to the EC level of zero. Thus, after the transition, U.S. soy farmers would be better off, not worse, they said.

On 21 March, a coalition of fourteen U.S. farm groups plus the huge Chamber of Commerce sent a joint letter to President Reagan. They blasted unilateral EC trade restrictions as "very serious threats to the health of American agriculture," and they urged him "to take action to ensure that American agriculture receives adequate compensation from the EC." They added that "failure to respond promptly and forcefully would weaken our opportunity to gain fair compensation."[18] Members of Congress were also warning the administration that the response had better be a firm one.

The U.S. Feed Grains Council, the lobby representing the most directly interested producers in Washington, was working up specific demands. Their preferred position was to ask the EC to compensate them by imposing a volume ceiling on EC subsidized grain exports, with the ceiling phasing down to zero over time.

DISCUSSION QUESTIONS

1. *Was the EC correct in stating that the treaties legally sanctioning the enlargement were negotiated over a period of six years and that the twelve ratifying*

parties thus have no obligation to obtain the consent of third-party trading partners? Even if legally correct, what ethical implications, if any, does the EC position hold?

2. *In terms of the process, could a more open and democratic means of reaching a consensus regarding trade concession changes have occurred? Why? Why not?*

3. *By disregarding the role the GATT plays in regulating and protecting its members' trade interests, both the EC and the United States were undermining the political legitimacy of that international regime. What are the political and ethical consequences of doing so for international affairs?*

4. *How should the EC or the United States weigh the immediate parochial interests of domestic farmers against long-term trade interests?*

THE U.S. ULTIMATUM AND EC OPTIONS, JUNE 1986

On 31 March 1986, President Reagan announced that the United States would slap the EC with trade sanctions soon unless it rescinded the quotas on oilseeds and grains in Portugal and provided adequate compensation for the higher tariffs in Spain. "We cannot allow the American farmer, once again, to pay the price for the European Community's enlargement," he declared.[19]

The office of the United States Trade Representative (USTR) issued a tentative list of EC products that would be the most likely victims.[20] They separated the Portuguese issues from the Spanish ones. In response to the 15 percent EC reservation of Portugal's grain market, the United States threatened to raise its tariffs on beer, chocolate, confectionery, and pear and apple juices by unspecified amounts. The EC quota on Portuguese oilseed imports was to trigger a tariff increase on white wine valued above $4.00 per gallon. These measures would take effect on 1 May unless the EC acted.

The deadline on the Spanish issues was set at 1 July. U.S. tariff increases would fall on a much longer list of goods, including white wine valued at less than $4.00 per gallon, brandy, cognac, mineral waters, a wide range of cheeses, whiskey, gin, hops, various meats and sausages, leather, potato starch, endives, carrots, olives, and coffee extracts. Again the exact amounts of the increases were left unspecified. Given such products as these, wags were soon dubbing the growing dispute "the Yuppie War."

The GATT requires that all restrictions be applied on an most-favored-nation basis. That is, U.S. tariff increases would affect all imports of the products hit, regardless of national origin. Wishing to observe that rule but not to harm suppliers other than the EC, U.S. officials thus struck from the list of EC exports all products of which other countries were significant suppliers.

They then carefully selected items that would concentrate pressure on France and also scatter it over most other EC member states. Almost half of the total burden would fall on French exports. White wine, one of the EC's leading exports to the United States, with sales valued at $204 million in 1985, came from France, Germany, and Italy. Brandy and cognac were major French exports, and their producers and distributors were known to be well organized politically. Cheese was another main export selected to put pressure on France and the Netherlands; whiskey and gin were selected to pressure Britain; and olives were chosen to apply pressure to the Mediterranean countries.

The aggregate EC export loss was intended to total about $1 billion, matching the value of estimated U.S. farm losses. The president's orders were set to take effect automatically on the two specified dates unless the EC were to act to satisfy the United States. Secretary of Agriculture Lyng explained that "our intention is to bring the EC to the negotiating table as soon as possible."[21]

This tough U.S. move, coming so suddenly in this case, was one of the most stunning steps the United States had taken in years of tussles with the EC. Retaliation had been threatened and used in other cases, but not before many rounds of discussion had taken place. Commissioner de Clercq in Brussels was outraged. "This confrontational approach risks leading to open commercial conflict even though the Community has declared itself ready to negotiate."[22] Later he snapped, "A European Community of 320 million people, conducting one-fifth of world trade, is not going to be pushed around."[23] The amounts of trade targeted would make this the most severe trade war ever fought between the EC and the United States.

On 9 April, the EC replied that it would be forced to counterretaliate if the Americans insisted on confrontation. The Commission approved a list of U.S. farm products that could be restricted. De Clercq told U.S. journalists in Brussels that "we do not like Rambo-style diplomacy. There is no reason to confront us with deadlines, with ultimatums." Professing a desire to settle the issue amicably under the GATT rules, he cautioned, "But I must underline our firm determination to defend the legitimate interests of the EC." Counter-retaliation would follow any U.S. measures "in complete symmetry."[24]

The Commission proposals would respond to U.S. retaliation against Portugal with surveillance of U.S. imports into the EC of corn, beer, wine, meat and edible offals, honey, foliage for bouquets, dried fruit, sunflower seeds, unrendered fats of bovine cattle, and fruit juice. In response to U.S. threats over Spain, the EC wheeled out three of the biggest cannons it had: counterthreats to restrict U.S. exports of corn gluten feed, wheat, and rice. In Washington, blows to these latter products were considered so serious that one congressman said they were equivalent to using a nuclear weapon in a trade war.

One reporter remarked, "The EEC [European Economic Community] list of products for retaliation appears to be designed to hit the US where it causes the most political pain."[25] The European Community, as the United States, chose its hit list carefully in its attempt to intimidate American farm groups.

A few days later, the United States reportedly indicated willingness to submit the Portugal issues to the GATT for a ruling. In Brussels, Deputy USTR Michael Smith told reporters, "We're trying to find ways of lowering the temperature without either side giving up its principles."[26] A precondition of the U.S. proposal was that the EC agree to suspend the phasing in of its measures in Portugal. In addition, the United States requested immediate "mini-XXIV:6 negotiations," limited to the EC and the United States and the Spanish issues.

The European Community rejected the U.S. proposal for mini-XXIV:6 negotiations, repeating their position that talks must be "global" in approach, and they also refused to agree to the suspension of EC measures in Portugal, for the same reasons given earlier. They did, however, authorize the Commission to negotiate in general over Spain.[27]

At this point, the member states had not yet come to a clear consensus on how to respond to U.S. "Ramboism." French Minister of Agriculture François Guillaume described the U.S. demands as "completely unacceptable"[28] and demanded that Brussels not cave in. West German Economics Minister Martin Bangemann warned, however, that "an escalation of trade restrictions" could "spill over into the industrial area with unforeseeable consequences for growth and employment . . . The Community should not take part in verbal muscle flexing, but should rather make unmistakably clear its readiness to negotiate and its interest in a settlement."[29]

When the EC Council met on 21 April to approve the Commission proposals, the French and Portuguese governments supported the Commission's approach without reservation, but they were the only states to be so enthusiastic. West Germany, Denmark, and the Netherlands were noticeably reticent about counterthreats.[30] Whatever difference they may have felt over responses, however, there was no serious division within the EC on the policy principle. All, including Margaret Thatcher's government in Britain, agreed that the United States was not entitled to special farm compensation.[31]

As the transatlantic tension thickened, domestic pressure mounted on both sides. In the United States, six senators cosponsored a resolution urging the president to use his full authority to retaliate unless the United States received full compensation, despite the EC counterthreat. California products were targeted for European retaliation. Meanwhile, in France the maize price was collapsing, and the French Association of Maize Producers (AGPM) was calling for members to sell surplus crops to the CAP authorities.

The EC, the United States, and other nations, throughout 1985 and 1986, were also attempting to commence a new multilateral round of GATT negotiations. On 15 April, GATT members agreed that their trade ministers would convene in Punta del Este, Uruguay, beginning 15 September to launch the round. Reform of agricultural policies was one of the central American objectives, and the EC also favored negotiations on a range of issues. Needless to say, however, a large-scale trade war between the two giants would cloud prospects for agreements in Uruguay or Geneva.

On 20 April, Clayton Yeutter, in Paris at the time, proposed to implement U.S. retaliation against Portugal in a way that would not actually hurt EC exporters right away if the EC would do likewise with the counterrestrictions it had threatened. He said lengthy administrative procedures would also prevent the U.S. measures from taking effect before 11 May. "We leaned over backwards,"[32] Yeutter maintained, hoping the delay would encourage a resolution. The move was also apparently designed to clear the charged atmosphere before the Tokyo economic summit, which was to be held at the beginning of May.

On 15 May, Reagan ordered Portugal-related quotas, not tariffs, and set the levels above the corresponding quantities exported in 1985, which avoided any immediate loss in European sales. De Clercq called this step "a pointless escalation." The next day, the EC began surveillance of the U.S. products it had selected on 9 April, but also without any restrictive effect.

On the one hand, some European officials urged freezing or even conceding the Portugal issues, feeling that the European Community had made a serious tactical error by inadvertently catching soybeans in particular in the first place. In Washington, the American Soybean Association was a particularly active force and was highly sensitive to the European market. In the farm trade business, one of the pillars of the status quo was a 1960s deal between the EC and the United States, whereby the latter accepted the CAP system in return for an EC guarantee that it would never impose a tariff on soybeans or corn gluten feed. This zero-duty commitment was the foundation that permitted huge subsequent U.S. soybean exports to the EC. Any question about the soybean zero binding or about applying it in new member states was sure to mobilize one of the most determined U.S. lobbies against the project.

On the other hand, a different European policymaker favored precisely the opposite tack—imposing or threatening a small tariff on soybeans and corn gluten feed in Iberia in order to create a bargaining chip that might be generously conceded later as a means of reaching agreement closer to EC preferences. He explained that "with a very low tariff, something like 0.006 percent, the press here would have said, 'well, this is nothing. The Americans are being unreasonable.' But on the other side, the ASA would have been very strongly opposed . . . I think we made a big mistake on this point. We should have done it so we would have some 'weapons.'"[33]

In the meantime, on 2 May the U.S. team had come forth with a new position on Spain. They asked the European Community for compensation in the form of a guarantee that the EC-12 as a whole would import 13.5 million metric tons of feed grains annually from all third parties, free of the variable levy.[34] The figure was calculated as an average of imports during a three-year period in the early 1980s, evidently adding a figure for losses in Spain to one for the EC-10. The proposal did not call for a quota for the United States alone because this would have clashed with Washington's general position in the GATT that attacked discriminatory and market-sharing schemes.

Most EC specialists regarded this U.S. demand for 13.5 million metric tons as outrageous. The French corn growers labeled it "grotesque," citing the fact that U.S. corn exports to Spain had been about 2.7 million metric tons in each of the last two seasons.[35] In fact, Brussels officials later recalled that the 13.5 million metric tons seemed so high as to indicate that the Reagan Administration was not serious about reaching an agreement at all, but instead might be bent on landing some commercial blows, perhaps for domestic political reasons as the November elections approached.

As June passed, negotiators became increasingly pessimistic about a resolution before that date. After 1 March, Spain had imported no more U.S. maize, switching instead to French maize, British barley, and EC feed wheat.[36] Lyng told reporters, "It may be inevitable that things will get worse before they get any better."[37] An extension of the 1 July deadline, he insisted, was impossible.

In Europe, COPA "urgently request[ed that] the Council take a firm and united stand in the face of American threats." It branded the U.S. action "totally unjustifiable and contrary to the rules of GATT." COPA reminded the Americans that the EC is the world's biggest importer of farm and food products and that it ran a considerable trade deficit in those products. The EC, it added pointedly, was also the single biggest customer of U.S. farmers.[38]

Meeting on 16 and 17 June, the EC states closed ranks in preparation for trade conflict. The Council decided that the Commission should target U.S. corn gluten feed, rice, and wheat at the same time as the U.S. measures were actually implemented. In late June one observer reported, "the mood on both sides is somber; positions are still so far apart that there is little basis for compromise."[39]

At this stage, no one in Brussels thought Washington was bluffing. It seemed clear that the United States would carry out its threat in the absence of concessions. Similarly, on the other side of the ocean, at least some U.S. negotiators believed that if it came to that, EC leaders would have little option politically but to carry out their own counterthreats. Brussels was probably not bluffing either. Each side was thinking about how to handle the situation after retaliation blows had fallen.

DISCUSSION QUESTIONS

1. *Were the retaliatory tariff measures necessary to bring the EC to the negotiating table?*
2. *Was the United States engaging in morally questionable means?*
3. *What were their effects on the gaining of a favorable U.S. resolution? Does the end justify the means?*
4. *When the United States first expressed its opposition to the changes in tariffs on agricultural products, the EC suggested that the GATT Commission mediate a negotiated settlement (under GATT Article XXIV:6). The United States rejected the suggestion because the GATT proceedings would take too long. However, a month later, after the United States had suddenly instituted retaliatory tariffs and the EC had countered with severe measures of its own the United States did suggest that the GATT hold "mini-XXIV:6 negotiations." Which ethical framework best explains the nature of the power plays and the subsequent compromise on the part of the United States?*

TEMPORARY TRUCE

The two sides continued their intensive negotiations right up to the deadline. On 1 July, Yeutter and de Clercq met in Washington for breakfast and last-minute bargaining. The two then boarded a plane for an overnight flight to Paris. What transpired during the flight was not disclosed, but as they exited the plane in Paris both seemed more optimistic than when they had departed. It was reported that the two had agreed to lay aside the Portugal issue until the following year, when U.S. farmers would first feel the effects of the EC restrictions. In the meantime they would concentrate on Spain, the larger market for the United States with the greater loss. Yeutter also announced in Paris that U.S. retaliation against Spain would actually take ten days to go into effect.

De Clercq's visit to Paris was no accident. During his stay he met with French Prime Minister Jacques Chirac and the French government.

Newspaper reports indicated that de Clercq tried to persuade Chirac that a temporary truce would be in everyone's interest.[40]

Evidently, de Clercq had proposed a temporary arrangement that would at least provide time for further negotiations. The EC offered to guarantee that it would import 208,000 tons of feed grains monthly until the end of the year if the United States would delay its threatened retaliation. The United States demanded 300,000 tons.[41]

One day later a "cease-fire" in the "Yuppie War" was reached. The EC increased its offer to 234,000 tons of feed grains per month, and the United States agreed to this temporary arrangement. The Common External Tariff would be applied in Spain as provided in the treaty. But the EC agreed to monitor U.S. sales of maize, sorghum, corn gluten feed, distillers' draft, and citrus pellets in Spain. If combined sales of these feed products dropped below 234,000 tons per month, the EC obligated itself to import the shortfall by permitting sales at a reduced levy, until 31 December 1986. The EC said the figure of 234,000 was the monthly average of the relevant U.S. exports in 1985. The value of this trade was estimated to be about $130 million.

The EC declared that these steps in no way called into question the Treaty of Accession or the principles of the CAP, nor did they prejudge the outcome of the XXIV:6 negotiations. Both the United States and the EC were committed to finding a lasting solution during the breathing space. It was also understood that if a permanent settlement was not found by 31 December, both sides would be free to go ahead with their retaliation plans.

In sum, the EC had decided in effect to accept U.S. grain that would not have been allowed under their Treaty of Accession, to make an exception to the principle of EC preference, and to grant Washington some sector-specific compensation, but all for only a six-month period. The U.S. government had agreed to postpone tough action temporarily, in return for compensation much smaller than it claimed. The United States also acknowledged grain substitutes as partial offsets.

By most accounts, neither side linked its behavior to the preparations for the Uruguay round in the sense of threatening to scuttle the GATT process if it did not win the bilateral dispute. Although each raised the argument that the other was putting the round in jeopardy, the Americans especially maintained that the bilateral dispute concerning the enforcement of the existing GATT rules; they would not consider "paying" in negotiations over new rules in order to get the EC to obey the old ones. Also, each side did not attempt to exploit NATO or other security issues as leverage. They kept the dispute on a relatively narrow track up to this point.

Although both negotiating teams hailed the time-buying settlement, farmers on both sides angrily blasted their representatives for weakness. On 4 July, the French Association of Maize Producers or AGPM, joined by other

French farm groups, mounted vocal demonstrations in Paris and dumped 2 tons of corn onto the streets in protest. They piled 10 more tons at the feet of a Paris replica of the American Statue of Liberty, whose centennial was being celebrated that day. The corn problem was not exactly front-page news in France, and the growers felt their interests were not being taken seriously enough.

They demanded to know why they should be the only Europeans to pay for EC enlargement. "This armistice," they declared, "presented as a temporary one, introduced for the first time in the history of the Community and its relations with the United States the grave precedent of a concession from one isolated sector rather than from agriculture and industry as a whole." They called it "a veritable Munich."[42] According to one source, the AGPM had urged the addition of at least the competing feeds besides corn to the list, thus perhaps reducing the amount of U.S. corn they would have to accept—which they saw as their only satisfaction in this agreement. Jacques Chaban-Delmas, president of the French National Assembly, and other French parliamentarians allied with him, insisted that France should not "subscribe to an accord which deprives the agriculture of the South-West—whose production of fruit and vegetables is gravely threatened by Spanish competition—of the only compensation it could hope for."[43] The AGPM estimated that the temporary accord would cost them about $540 million in lost revenue.[44]

The French government had reportedly eased its resistance only on 3 July, the very day the deal was announced.[45] Rumors had it that France would yield only if the EC was prepared to pay restitutions to finance exports of French corn outside of the EC that otherwise would have been sold in Spain.[46] Reportedly during the 2 July EC meeting when de Clercq presented the truce to the EC ambassadors, the Commission made a general declaration that it would take any measures necessary to prevent the arrangement from having harmful consequences, but no more specific commitment was made formally. The EC did begin such subsidized corn exports within a few months.[47]

Community-wide farm organizations added their voices to the outcry. COPA denounced "this unbalanced agreement to the detriment of the EC," complaining that it "puts at stake the principle of community preference." They demanded a definitive solution "on the basis of the globality approach as set out by the Council, and by fully re-establishing Community preference in the enlarged Community."[48]

The Spanish government was also disappointed with the agreement, but from the importing side. All along it had felt like a pawn in the struggle between the two trading superpowers. Spain argued that in the event the EC needed to purchase grain at a reduced-levy, these special imports should be made available only to Spain, and not to the entire European Community. The EC Commission, however, had refused to accept the Spanish position.

Later recalling the decision to accept this temporary settlement, one Brussels negotiator said:

> Once we realized that there was a risk of a major trade war and possible strains on cohesion in the Community—our tendencies were far from unanimous—we saw that probably we would not have success- fully resisted a trade war. It was decided that it would be better to drop something on the table, something limited, that would not pre- judge our position later, but would allow time for people to realize what such a thing was a possibility.

U.S. farmers were equally angry. Their representative had informed U.S. negotiators that "any agreement that does not fully compensate the producers of corn and sorghum who have lost access to the markets of Spain and Portugal, will be unacceptable to the U.S. Feed Grains Council and our members."[49] They had estimated full compensation for Spain at around $600 million worth of annual sales. The interim agreement, however, provided less than half of what they claimed to lose. The Council denounced the temporary settlement as "a bitter pill to swallow."[50]

In Geneva, at the end of July, the French government—with support from Spain, Greece, and Ireland—refused to accept the proposed agenda text for the new round, a text that had the support of most EC members. France wanted to deflect discussion away from export subsidies and to ensure that agriculture talks would be held separately from those on other sectors so as to prevent trade-offs between sectors.[51] Clayton Yeutter, for his part, soon threatened that, should U.S. demands not be met, the U.S. delegation would walk out of Punta del Este.

In August 1986, Yeutter and de Clercq negotiated a truce in the citrus-pasta dispute. The provisional agreement involved larger EC tariff quotas for four citrus products in return for U.S. agreement to reduce to tariffs on six products and not to challenge EC preferential accords further.[52] COPA denounced this draft agreement as another assault on EC preference, and, because it gave no real compensation to EC regions affected by the concessions to the United States, COPA insisted that "a very firm attitude must be adopted towards a trading partner who is attempting by all possible means to undermine certain basic principles and instruments of the Common Agricultural Policy, which may lead to its destruction."[53]

At the Punta del Este conference in September, tough bargaining lasted until early morning hours, and tempers became frayed. In the end, agreement was reached, including terms for future agriculture talks that both the EC and the United States could accept.

Meanwhile, however, other European interests likely to be affected by a trade war also made their voices heard, though usually behind closed doors. In France, cognac was the largest item on the U.S. hit list in terms of trade value, and it needed no subsidy. When cognac producers made their quiet contacts, the French government assured them that in the end the Americans would not go through with their threats. The corn growers were more visible, but by themselves were not a large force in French politics.

"Some of the biggest pressures on the Commission to reach a settlement came from the industrial people, people like Volkswagen and whiskey, who were very afraid of a trade war," according to a well-informed participant in Brussels. The German government pressed hard for a settlement, for security as well as for economic reasons. The Germans also worked to prevent compensation from taking the form of greater imports of U.S. industrial goods.

Another well-placed participant reports that the French government's hard-line position against any permanent concessions softened in private in October 1986. They "wanted to avoid a major break with Germany." The Germans had worked quite closely with the French at Punta del Este. The French were pleased by that, and "a trade war with the United States would have upset the Germans very much." The Chirac government had made close ties with West Germany a central policy theme.

The November elections did not go well for the Reagan administration. Although the president campaigned hard for the reelection of republican senators, voters still took control of the Senate away from his party.

In any case, when trans-Atlantic talks over the Yuppie War resumed, the U.S. and EC positions had not changed in substance from their respective stands at the outbreak. Negotiators on both sides had drawn heavy criticism at home for having negotiated away farmers' rights during the interim agreement. At the end of November, de Clercq told a conference in Antwerp that "negotiations over the issue so far have been painful" and that the EC and the United States remained "diametrically opposed."[54]

By November, it was also evident that EC feed grain imports were not reaching the 234,000 tons monthly promised in the interim agreement. The United States accused the EC of manipulating its levy system so as to keep U.S. feed grains out of Spain without overtly reneging on the interim agreement. EC officials blamed low commercial bids at the weekly tenders for the shortfall. The Commission proposed that the EC purchase the shortfall during the remainder of the year.[55] Eventually the grain did move in agreed upon quantities.

Late in November, the AGPM sent a delegation to Washington to underline the seriousness of their situation. They raised the idea of a solution in which the EC would limit subsidized feed grain exports to third countries, rather than guarantee access of U.S. corn exports to Spain.[56] European farm leaders said it seemed irrational for all concerned for the EC to import more U.S. grain and turn around and reexport the equivalent to third countries, where it would displace other U.S. sales. Thus, the EC ends up footing the bill via reduced import levies and greater export restitutions, and yet U.S. farmers are not better off worldwide.

Limits on EC subsidized exports had also been the top demand of the U.S. Feed Grains Council. To Washington officials, however, this approach would mean compromising their principle that the GATT obliged the EC to pay sector-specific compensation in Europe. Washington would also see this solution as an agreement that the EC could pay compensation by agreeing not to do something it was not supposed to do in the first place.

At the same time, the French corn growers threatened to file a counter-vailing duty suit against U.S. corn exporters if the eventual agreement proved unsatisfactory from their point of view. Canada had just imposed such a duty on U.S. corn, and the French delegation flew to Ontario to compare notes. "European corn producers are threatened in their survival, and the only solution would be to file a countervailing duty case such as Canada's," said the president of the AGPM.[57]

In early December, the United States reduced its claim for losses in Spain from an estimated $500 or $600 million to $400 million. U.S. negotiators explained this was as a consequence of the recalculation of the base period for estimating trade value, after they had received an additional year's data on U.S. exports to Spain.

As the 31 December deadline drew nearer, farm interests on each side of the Atlantic kept pressure on their negotiators to remain firm. With only three weeks left until the deadline, a reporter remarked that "agreement is no closer than when the mess started a year ago."

DISCUSSION QUESTIONS

1. When membership in an institution such as the United Nations or GATT is voluntary, the political legitimacy of the institution depends upon the cooperative will of each member state. Why should country representatives set aside parochial domestic interests and work for a compromise within the framework of GATT?

2. According to the communitarian view, what objectives and principles ought to guide the working out of international trade disputes?

3. In a globally interdependent world, what value does the EC's communitarian views have in protecting its member-nations interests?

REACHING A COMPROMISE

Lyng and Yeutter flew to Brussels for another round of negotiations on 12 and 13 December. Outside the vast EC headquarters building, European corn farmers marched with huge banners, and EC political leaders continued to maintain quite a firm posture. Inside, the EC proposed a four-year agreement in which it would guarantee imports of 1.6 million metric tons per year of maize and sorghum into Spain from third countries. This estimate took account of rising Spanish production as well as the projected shift to cereal substitutes.

The two sides were both now talking about compensation largely in agriculture. The Americans, however, said that they could not accept less than 4.4 million metric tons annually, for an indefinite period. To de Clercq, this U.S. position was "economically, politically, and psychologically unreasonable. It would have created another food mountain [in the EC]." With the two sides still miles apart, the Brussels talks broke down.[58]

EC negotiators next approached the U.S. side with a request to extend the 31 December deadline by one month. After a meeting of the president's Economic Policy Council, however, the administration refused.

On 30 December, President Reagan announced that the United States would impose retaliatory 200 percent duties on about $400 million worth of European brandy, white wine, gin, cheeses, canned ham, olives, and other goods. French brandy and wine would account for $250 million of the total. "The intention is to stop that trade in its tracks," Yeutter mentioned. At the same time, he noted that hearings would be held on the final product list, and that the penalties would not actually take effect until perhaps the end of January. The EC repeated that it would impose countermeasures in that event.[59]

On 2 January 1987, the *Washington Post* reported that U.S. demands were at 3 million tons of feedgrains annually. Another bargaining session was scheduled for 22 January.

On 8 January, de Clercq met with the EC's Council of Permanent Representatives (COREPER) in Brussels to discuss the EC option. The French representative argued that the EC should not compromise its external tariff system by giving in to U.S. threats. The French government had struck the same chord a few days earlier when it had informed the Commission that there could be no further concessions on the Iberian access dispute. The Dutch representative, supported by his German counterpart, expressed reservations over a continuation to hold firm. Both the Netherlands and Germany were the main importers of U.S. corn gluten feed and were concerned about the availability of alternatives. One European newspaper did report rumors that the EC was prepared to make "substantial concessions."[60]

On the same day, Clayton Yeutter announced that his government had always been willing to consider any trade benefits it would receive from lower industrial tariffs arising from the EC enlargement. The United States was now willing to accept some of the $400 million it demanded in the form of additional industrial sales, but most of the compensation would still have to come in the farm sector.[61]

On 22 January, de Clercq met with Yeutter and Lyng in Washington one more time. Despite the apparent softening in both sides' positions, they deadlocked again. De Clercq flew back to Brussels on the night of 24 January, and no further meetings between the top negotiators were scheduled.

With no resolution in sight, exporters and importers on both sides of the Atlantic were now hurriedly preparing for the war. Panicky French cognac producers chartered Air France planes to rush as much product into the United States as possible before the drawbridge went up. They planned to follow by exporting less expensive cognac because U.S. retaliatory duties applied only to brandy costing more than $13 a gallon. Danish farmers were planning to export bigger hams because penalties applied only to hams weighing three pounds or less.

Alerted now by extensive news coverage, yuppies in the United States began to fear the worst. The new duties would raise the price of French brie from $5.99 a pound to $14. A bottle of Italian table wine was going to cost $5.00 instead of $2.99.

By now it had become clear in Europe that Washington was at least serious about the possibility of agreement, rather than welcoming a trade war. Washington had reduced the dollar value of its claims, and in January had raised the possibility of industrial compensation. It was equally clear, though, that retaliation was on its way if Washington could not be satisfied at the table.

With only five days remaining, COREPER agreed to a significant increase in the EC offer, from 1.6 to 2.2. million tons of feedgrains, assuming some U.S. flexibility. In particular, the U.S. side agreed that imports of nongrain feeds could be counted against the quota.

With one day left before the U.S. blows would fall, the two negotiating teams, in the absence of their chief, continued wrestling until 3 o'clock in the morning of 29 January. The U.S. side was led by Ambassador Alan Woods, deputy USTR, and the EC side by directorate-general-I Commission official Roderick Abbott. De Clercq and Yeutter spent the night on transatlantic telephones. Finally at mid-morning on 29 January, the two teams shook hands over an agreement.

The accord reiterated that neither side had accepted the other's interpretation of the GATT compensation requirement. But the United States agreed to suspend its retaliatory measures in return for an EC guarantee that Spain would import at least 2 million metric tons of corn and 300,000 metric tons of sorghum from third countries each year for the next four years. The United States agreed that imports of three nongrain feeds would be deducted from these quantities. The Americans expected to get about two-thirds of the guaranteed purchases. In addition, Brussels extended its zero-duty binding on soybean products and corn gluten feed to Spain and Portugal, and it gave up its 15 percent preferential corner in Portugal's grain import market. This last concession meant that an estimated 400,000 to 450,000 metric tons of U.S. cereals could be sold in Portugal. The agreement further included a reduction of EC import duties on some 26 industrial and other products for the entire European Community market. Officials were not sure how much industrial sales would rise. Finally, the two sides would meet again in mid-1990 to review the situation at that time. Neither changed its nonrestrictive measures related to the Portuguese soybean regime. USTR valued the European concessions at about $400 million.

The EC approved the agreement only after a lengthy debate and despite strong objections from Spain. Since the summer, Madrid had become more concerned with the implications for Spanish farmers and had switched its position in Brussels from the consumer to the producer side. The agreement directed the imports to Spain, and the Commission planned to prevent them from being reexported to other EC countries, as Spain had wanted in July. Now although the Spanish did not oppose an import commitment as such, they wanted the commitment to be "Communitized," fearing that the U.S. corn would lower domestic prices. At a COREPER meeting, the Spanish ambassador insisted that either the quota had to be shared or the agreement had to be renegotiated to cut the size of U.S. imports into Spain. No other government supported him, however. Only after receiving assurances that its markets would be protected did Spain grudgingly assent, the last member to do so.[62]

Farm lobbyists in both the United States and the EC again vigorously denounced their representatives' decisions. The National Corn Growers Association complained, "At a time when our U.S. corn farmers are under severe economic pressure, it is inconceivable that our government would accept such an agreement. . . . They [the U.S. negotiators] should have walked away from the agreement before they got to this stage. We may have needed a little trade war."[63] A Feed Grains Council leader noted, "The terms of the agreement are less favorable than those contained in the July interim agreement. No one in the U.S. feed grains sector was satisfied with the interim agreement, so I don't see how they could be satisfied with the terms of the new agreement."[64]

Deputy USTR Alan Woods responded saying, "You have to remember that retaliation would not have resulted in the sale of one more kernel of corn to Spain or Portugal."[65] Richard Lyng defended the outcome by emphasizing that "this is the first time that the United States has received full compensation following enlargement of the EC."[66] Yeutter told U.S. corn farmers, "I find it hard to believe that we could have been any more firm than we were in that particular negotiation . . . As I value the [EC] commitments, they are about 80 percent in the feedgrains area . . . I really believe we pushed the feedgrains compensation about as far as we possibly could. As you may know, the Community debated the agreement for 11 hours before finally approving it."[67]

On the European side, de Clercq also said he considered himself satisfied that an equitable resolution had been found. "It is an honorable compromise, which allows us to avoid a trade war which would have caused the two parties damage without precedent."

European farm lobbies were as outraged as were the Americans. COPA called the settlement "another serious blow to the principle of community preference." It would give access to foreign maize and sorghum "under preferential conditions" and renounced a provision of the Treaty of Adhesion. The import commitments would "entail very heavy costs to the already strained Community budget and will cause serious problems to the Community cereals' market." COPA "can in no circumstances accept that European farmers be the ones to have to bear the financial costs of these preferential imports."[68]

In Geneva on 29 January, the EC rejected the Punta del Este negotiation program on agriculture. The head of the EC delegation explained that the rejection was a result of the heavy price the EC had to pay to settle the Yuppie War. The EC could not be expected to pay a further price by bowing to U.S. insistence that the GATT negotiations on agriculture be put on the fast track.[69]

The fundamental problems that lay at the heart of the Yuppie War—policies on both sides encouraging surplus farm production and export subsidies—remained as far from resolution as ever. Only a month later, the EC began the subsidized export of French corn to North Africa, irking U.S. farmers anew.

DISCUSSION QUESTIONS

1. *What were the larger issues at stake if an agreement had not been reached?*
2. *Did the French farm growers have a legitimate claim in that they unfairly paid the burden for the EC's enlargement? Were they "sold out" in the negotiations in order to minimize the potential for a full-scale trade war?*
3. *The trade dispute was ultimately resolved without the assistance of GATT. What does this say about the nature of international institutions in contemporary international affairs? What does this say about the role of ethics in international relations?*

4. *Is the agreement proof that the sum of the benefits to the two parties was greater than going it alone to attain national gains? Could the United States or the EC have gone it alone?*

5. *To what extent are the lessons peculiar to dealings with the EC and the United States? To what extent do the lessons generalize to other international issues such as the Law of the Sea?*

NOTES

1. Letter from U.S. Feed Grains Council to U.S. Dept. of Agriculture, 20 June 1986.

2. *Washington Post*, 19 July 1986.

3. *International Trade Reporter*, 26 March 1986.

4. *International Trade Reporter*, 26 February 1986.

5. "The Citrus-Pasta Dispute between the United States and the European Community," Report 87-911 ENR, U.S. Congressional Reference Service, November 1987; *Agra Europe*, 1 August 1986.

6. *Agra Europe*, 23 May 1986.

7. EC exports including intra-EC trade came to 36 percent of world trade in 1985. IMF, *Directory of Trade Statistics*, 1986 Yearbook.

8. EC Commission, *The Agricultural Situation in the Community*, 1985 Report.

9. Interview conducted by John Odell in Brussels with an influential farm leader, June 1988.

10. Interviews conducted by John Odell with European officials and farm leaders, June 1988.

11. Interviews conducted by John Odell with Bernard Valluis, Director, Association of Maize Producers, Paris, France, 20 June 1988.

12. Association General des Producteurs de Mais, *Rapport D'Orientation* 1986, p. 5.

13. Delegation of the EC Commission in Washington, "Letter from Europe, " 24 March 1986.

14. Interview conducted by John Odell in Washington, D.C. with a European official, 3 June 1988.

15. Interview conducted by John Odell with a European negotiator, June 1988.

16. *International Trade Reporter*, 12 March 1986.

17. *European Community News*, 17 June 1986.

18. *Letter from National Grange*, 21 March 1986.

19. *Agra Europe*, 11 April 1986.

20. *Agra Europe*, 4 April 1986.

21. Letter to U.S. Feed Grains Council, 15 April 1986.

22. *European Community News*, 31 March 1986.

23. *Europe*, June 1986.

24. *International Trade Reporter*, 16 April 1986.

25. *Agra Europe*, 20 June 1986.

26. *International Trade Reporter*, 16 April 1986.

27. *International Trade Reporter*, 23 April 1986.

28. *Agra Europe*, 4 April 1986.

29. *International Trade Reporter*, 16 April 1986.

30. G. N. Yannopoulos, *Customs Unions and Trade Conflicts: The Enlargement of the European Community* (London: Routledge, 1988), p. 122.

31. Interviews conducted by John Odell in Brussels and London, June and July 1988.

32. *International Trade Reporter*, 23 April 1986.

33. Interview conducted by John Odell in Brussels, June 1988.

34. Letter from U.S. Dept. of Agriculture to U.S. Feed Grains Council, 29 May 1986; letter from U.S. Feed Grains Council to U.S. Dept. of Agriculture, 29 June 1986.

35. AGPM, *Rapport D'Orientation*, 1986.

36. *Agra Europe*, 11 July 1986.

37. *Agra Europe*, 20 June 1986.

38. Press releases, Brussels, 3 April and 16 June 1986.

39. *Agra Europe*, 20 June 1986.

40. *Financial Times*, 3 July 1986.

41. *International Trade Reporter*, 9 July 1986.

42. *Le Monde*, 5 July 1986.

43. *Le Monde*, 4 July 1986.

44. *International Trade Reporter*, 9 July 1986.

45. *Le Monde*, 4 July 1986.

46. *Agra Europe*, 4 July 1986.

47. Interviews conducted by John Odell in Brussels and Paris, June and July 1988.

48. Press release, Brussels, 11 July 1986.

49. Letter from U.S. Feed Grains Council to Clayton Yeutter, 25 April 1986.

50. Letter from U.S. Feed Grains Council to Clayton Yeutter, 8 October 1986.

51. *Agra Europe*, 1 August 1986 and 19 September 1986.

52. "The Citrus-Pasta Dispute," see note 5.

53. Press release, Brussels, 12 September 1986.

54. *International Trade Reporter*, 21 November 1986.

55. *Agra Europe*, 5 December 1986.

56. *Ibid.*

57. *International Trade Reporter*, 3 December 1986.

58. *International Trade Reporter,* 17 December 1986.

59. *New York Times, Wall Street Journal,* 31 December 1986.

60. *Agra Europe,* 9 January 1987.

61. *Ibid.*

62. Interview conducted by John Odell in Brussels, June 1988.

63. Letter from National Corn Growers Association, 30 January 1987.

64. Letter from U.S. Freed Grains Council, 2 February 1987.

65. USTR letter from U.S. Feed Grains Council.

66. Press release, 29 January 1987.

67. Letter, Yeutter to NCGA, 13 February 1987. Later an American negotiator noted that it was actually helpful for their domestic lobbyists to complain that they would have preferred a trade war. If the EC asked for greater restrictions in the future, "we can point to this pressure and say we can't possibly do that."

68. Press release, Brussels, 30 January 1987.

69. *Washington Post,* 29 January 1987.

7

PRESERVING THE RAIN FOREST: BRAZIL AND THE "INTERNATIONALIZATION" OF AMAZONIA

In the UNCLOS case, we saw how national interests and political expediency thwarted efforts to reach an agreement on distributive justice issues regarding the use of a global commons. In the GATT case we saw how two member-nations snubbed that regime's authority. Yet they cooperated and compromised when their individual pursuits of their own bargaining ends had resulted in the meeting of no one's. This case is different from the previous cases in that, to date, there exists no international regime on rain forests and rain forests; are found within the borders of a country—they are not a global commons in the sense that the atmosphere or the open seas are.

Regardless of the fact that the Amazonian rain forest belongs to Brazil, other nations and nonprofit environmental organizations have successfully pressured that nation into making the preservation of the rain forest an international priority. This case study examines the distributive justice claims

This chapter is a revised version of the case study by Rachel McCleary, Development Strategies in Conflict: Brazil and the Future of the Amazon, *Carnegie Council on Ethics and International Affairs case study no. 1 and Pew case study no. 501.*

outsiders have made to the preservation of the Amazonian rain forest. Who has a right to benefit from the rain forest and in what way? If outsiders have a recognized moral claim to the preservation of the Amazonian rain forest, then what do they owe Brazilians who rely on it for a living? What obligation do outsiders have to assist Brazil in maintaining it as a renewable resource?

The second set of questions this case study raises is in regard to political legitimacy and sovereignty. Brazil has argued that outsiders have no moral claim to Amazonia. The rain forest is found within Brazil's borders, and sovereignty over territory is a fundamental concept of international law and the United Nations system. If certain natural resources found within a country's borders are common goods in some sense, then perhaps the restrictive notions of sovereignty and property rights need to be replaced with a standard of distributive justice that adequately addresses global responsibility for environmental degradation.

* * *

Contemporary Brazil is facing social and economic problems of immense proportions. It is experiencing a population explosion—with an estimated growth from 153 million people in 1991 to more than 210 million people in the year 2011.[1] Brazil's economy is experiencing hyperinflation and the largest external debt in the developing world, $110 billion. Within Brazilian society, there exists extreme inequality in the distribution of land and income. The rural poor make up the largest segment of Brazilian society. Yet 70 percent of rural households do not own the land they farm. It is estimated that 4.5 percent of Brazil's landowners own 81 percent of the farmland.

To address these problems, Brazil has looked to the Amazon region for solutions. The natural tropical forest areas known as the Amazon cover 5.5 million square kilometers in nine South American countries. The Amazon rain forest is the world's largest contiguous tropical moist forest, and 3.8 million square kilometers of it are found within the borders of Brazil. This geographic area constitutes 58 percent of Brazil's territory and is commonly referred to as "Amazonia."[2] (See Figure 7.1)

Members of the international community recognize that Brazil is facing huge domestic problems. These countries and their citizens, nonetheless, argue against Brazil's depletion of the rain forest on the ground that it is a common good. As a global resource it is the largest part of the last remaining contiguous tropical moist forest in the world, and its destruction is significantly diminishing the quality of life on earth in three ways.

First, the deforestation is degrading the local and regional ecological system. Without the density of standing trees that make up the rain forest, exposed topsoil is washed away by water or blown away by winds. The root systems of a rain forest help to reduce flooding and landslides, and keep sediment out of rivers and reservoirs. In addition, a rain forest serves to filter and purify the water in streams, underground water systems, and springs.

FIGURE 7.1 Brazil

Source: W. Raymond Duncan and Carolyn McGiffert Ekedahl, *Moscow and the Third World Under Gorbachev* (Boulder: Westview Press, 1990), p. 192.

Second, the destruction of the rain forest is eliminating the habitats of large numbers of species for whom the rain forest is home. Several millions of plant and animal species live in the rain forest. The World Resources Institute estimates that between 1990 and 2020 deforestation of tropical rain forests will result in the loss of approximately 5 to 15 percent of the world's species. The extinction of these species, at the rate of 15,000 to 50,000 a year, represents the loss of genetic diversity.

The loss of genetic diversity means that species with potential future value as foods, medicines, and industrial products are disappearing permanently. Regardless of their contribution to human welfare, however, the extinction of species represents the loss of an irreplaceable good—the diversity of life on earth. As two researchers, M. E. Soule and B. A. Wilcox, express it, "Death is one thing; an end to birth is something else."

Third, the severe depletion of the rain forest is contributing to the greenhouse effect. Tropical rain forests and the organic matter found in their soils contains 20 percent of the earth's carbon pool. When the forests are destroyed, the carbon is released into the atmosphere in the form of carbon dioxide. Molecules of carbon dioxide absorb infrared radiation, causing the radiation to be trapped in the earth's atmosphere. This in turn produces an increase in the average global temperature. The warming of the earth's atmosphere can have potentially disastrous effects not only on human welfare but on plant and animal life as well.

Scientists are predicting that global warming will lead to a rise in sea levels, causing flooding. Global warming will also produce changes in rainfall distribution, which in turn will alter soil chemistry and have a direct impact on plant and animal life.

The Brazilian government has argued that if Amazonia is not exploited, Brazil has no other way to produce goods (e.g., steel) for export on the international market, to industrialize in order to attract foreign capital, to provide land and food for its population, nor to develop hydroelectric energy. With continued emphasis on market-oriented economic reforms in the Brady Plan, Brazil will continue to integrate Amazonia into its national economy.[3] The president of Brazil, Fernando Collor de Mello, is implementing a national economic policy along the lines suggested by the Brady Plan. State enterprises, such as steel manufacturing, are being sold to attract badly needed foreign investment. The issue for Brazilians is not whether Amazonia will be developed, but how quickly and to whose benefit.

Brazil (as do other nations) maintains that it has the sovereign right to do as it sees fit with the natural resources found within its borders. The Brazilian government claims that "the Amazon is ours . . . After all, it is situated in our territory."[4] Former president Jose Sarney refused to participate in the international environmental conference held at the Hague in March 1989. He saw the discussion of Amazonia by representatives of other nations as "a breach of sovereignty."[5] For Brazil, the development of Amazonia is a domestic issue, and not an international one. Does Brazil have the sovereign right to do as it sees fit with Amazonia?

Since their beginnings in the 1950s, Brazil's development strategies for Amazonia have been designed for the integration of the tropical rain forest areas into the national economy. This has been carried out by the systematic exploitation of the natural resources and by the conversion of the rain forest into land for small farmers and entrepreneurs. Frontier expansion in Amazonia, since the 1960s, is best characterized as a shift away from an implicitly recognized occupation of the forest areas to appropriation on the basis of legal ownership. This shift marks the transition from publicly held lands to private ownership, from the exploitation of natural resources within the forest to the cutting down of the forest in order to use the land.

These trends in development indicate that it is no longer possible to consider issues of deforestation separately from the development strategies implemented in Brazil's Amazonia. Given these development trends, it must be considered whether or not environmental conservation in Amazonia is a luxury that developing nations, such as Brazil, cannot afford.

DISCUSSION QUESTIONS

1. *How is the loss of a species "an end to birth"? Is this a significant argument for preserving rain forests? Another way of looking at this question is to ask yourself: If an animal or plant species does not benefit humanity in some tangible way, is it worth preserving?*
2. *Are environmental issues ultimately at odds with the development goals of a country such as Brazil?*
3. *What right do industrialized countries such as the United States have to put pressure on Brazil to preserve the rain forest when industrialized countries have not preserved their own forests?*
4. *Does justice require that people living in the industrialized countries begin to implement policies that will lower their material expectations and alter their living patterns in order to show Brazilians and other natural resource-rich countries that industrialized countries are serious about environmental preservation?*

CAUSES OF DEFORESTATION

The rate of conversion of Amazonian rain forest into grassland is itself a source of considerable controversy. The National Space Research Institute of Brazil (INPE) recently collected data showing that 7 percent of Legal Amazonia is deforested.[6] In 1988, the World Bank estimated that 12 percent of Amazonia is deforested.[7] The discrepancy in these interpretations is attributed to the method of determining deforestation. The INPE study relied on space photographs of smoke from the burning of the forest, which does not account for other deforestation methods. The World Bank estimate was based on a similar type of photography provided by the U.S. National Oceanic and Atmospheric Administration. But the World Bank estimate included data on deforestation caused by methods other than fire.

The causes of tropical deforestation vary according to the regions in Amazonia. However, experts agree that agriculture, both in the form of small-scale farming and cattle ranching, is the most significant cause.

Colonizing Amazonia

The government of Brazil has specifically instituted programs that were designed to attract small-scale farmers to Amazonia from other regions of Brazil. In 1970, the Brazilian government established the National Integration Program (PIN). The goal of the program was to settle 70,000 families in the Amazonian state of Pará, along the Trans-Amazon Highway that had yet to be constructed. PIN was established to address the needs of tens of thousands of people left homeless by a severe drought that occurred in 1969 in the northeast part of Brazil. These people were migrating to the coastal cities of Recife and João Pessoa, which were ill-equipped to handle such a large influx of people.

As part of PIN, the government offered to provide land in the state of Pará at a minimal cost to anyone who would come. In its publicity announcements for PIN, the government advertised fertile lands for farming. The development of the tropical forest area in Pará meant that there was a shift from large areas of public lands and areas occupied by Amerindians to areas of private ownership. Whereas the Amerindians had treated the rain forest as a renewable resource, the government was now establishing a program that directly encouraged people to cut down the forest in order to use the land for farming.

In 1972, the government completed the initial 1,200 kilometers of the Trans-Amazon Highway (which intersected the Belém-Brasilia Highway and the Cuiabá-Santarém Highway. (See Figure 7.2.) Immigrants who arrived were offered a 100-hectare plot classified as "terra rosa" soils, which were considered to be types of fertile soils. The settlers received credit and a ready-made house located either along the highway or in a planned community. Feeder roads were to be constructed, linking farms to markets; public schools and medical services were to be provided; and the government guaranteed to purchase the settlers' produce.

By the end of 1974, however, only 5,700 families had been settled along the Trans-Amazon Highway. Many things had gone wrong. First, the government officials who were supposed to identify fertile soils and allocate plots accordingly, could not keep up with the surge of immigrants seeking land. The officials were forced to abandon distribution of land based on the fertility of the soils. Farmers who chose plots with poor soils found that they could not produce food. They became indebted without viable means of

FIGURE 7.2 Roads and Colonization in the Brazilian Amazon

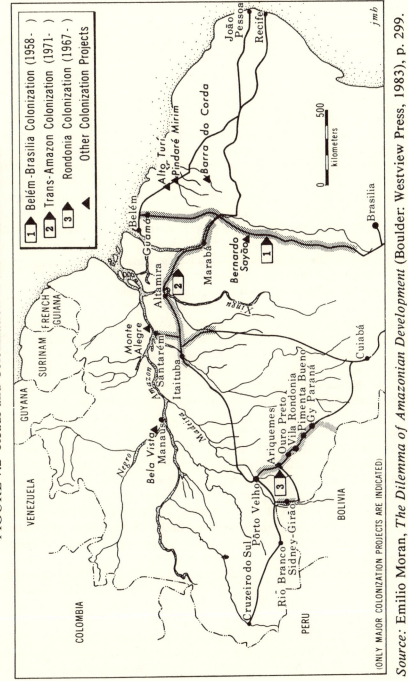

Source: Emilio Moran, *The Dilemma of Amazonian Development* (Boulder: Westview Press, 1983), p. 299.

becoming successful agricultural producers. In order to eke out a living, the settlers began burning more of the forest.

Second, government officials gave preference to families from the northeast without regard for their past success in agricultural production. Families were selected based on their size, their income, and the number of years they had been farmers.

Third, the construction of the main road cost three times the initially projected cost. As a result, the number of feeder roads to be built was reduced. Without these feeder roads, farmers could not transport their crops to urban markets; seasonal laborers could not make it to the farms to help with the harvest; and the long trips to town, coupled with bureaucratic tardiness, discouraged small farmers from applying for definitive title to their land. In addition, small farmers who participated in the colonization scheme experienced difficulty in obtaining investment credit if they did not possess clear title to their land. Cadastral officers were slow in processing land titles. They were also underpaid and easily bribed. Large landowners took advantage of the situation by intimidating small farmers or by forcibly removing them from their land. In the state of Pará, this expulsion of small farmers by large landowners led, oftentimes, to violent conflicts.

The ecological impact of PIN was restricted to certain areas of central Pará. First, because the planned feeder roads were not built, the human population was concentrated along the main roads. Second, the soils along that segment of the Trans-Amazon Highway proved to be primarily of poor quality. Furthermore, no valuable minerals were found by speculators.

In 1980, the Brazilian government instituted the Polonoroeste Project, the largest colonization scheme in Amazonia. Since the completion of the Cuiabá-Pôrto Velho Highway in 1968 (Figure 7.2), people began migrating spontaneously to the state of Rondônia. In the 1960s, about 3,000 people per year migrated to Rondônia. In the 1970s, it is estimated that 30,000 people migrated per year to that state. Unlike the PIN program, the government did not have to actively recruit migrants to the area. There are two reasons for the spontaneous migration to Rondônia. First, the construction of a highway means easier access to lands. The lands in Rondônia are more consistently fertile than those found in the state of Pará. Through word of mouth and government publicity, small farmers throughout Brazil learned of Rondônia and migrated. Second, it is estimated that during the 1970s and early 1980s, 25 to 30 percent of those small farmers came from the southern state of Paraná. The small coffee farms in Paraná, through subsidized credit, were being converted into mechanized soybean farms. Small farmers found that they could neither convert to mechanization nor could they continue to support their families on a small plot of farmland.

In the 1970s, the government established seven colonization projects along the Cuiabá-Pôrto Velho Highway for the population that had moved there spontaneously. By the end of the 1970s, however, the numbers of people moving into the area overtaxed the capacity of the government to control the clearing and burning of the forest. By 1980, the environmental destruction due to uncontrolled, spontaneous migration to the state was severe, and the government was forced to act.

With funding from the World Bank, the Brazilian government implemented the Polonoroeste Project. The Cuiabá-Pôrto Velho Highway was paved, and feeder roads were constructed so that farmers could get their produce out during the rainy season. Thirty-nine new colonization sites were designated. Like PIN, the numbers of immigrants strained the region's administrative capacities. Designated areas to be exempt from settlement, such as Amerindian reserves and forest preserves, were ignored.

Out of concern for the estimated 8,000 Amerindians living the project's designated area, international organizations began pressuring the World Bank to place environmental and social conditions on its funding for Polonoroeste. (See Figure 7.3.) The groups called for adequate demarcation and protection of fifteen Amerindian reserves, the implementation of public health measures to protect the Amerindians from such diseases as malaria, and to designate certain areas as biological reserves.

In 1984, thirty indigenous people's rights groups and environmental groups in the United States, Brazil, and Europe protested to the World Bank the continued disregard on the part of the Brazilian government for the Amerindians and the environment in and around Polonoroeste. In March 1985, the World Bank suspended funding until the Brazilian government took measures to identify and protect Amerindian reserves and biological reserves. These measures have led to the proposed Rondônia Natural Resources Management Project. The purpose of this state body is to look at the continuing need to specify and enforce environmental protection, to maintain monitoring capabilities, and to keep in check deforestation, illegal mining activities, squatting, and illegal invasions of conservation areas and Amerindian reserves.

Cattle Ranching

Cattle ranching is the most widespread form of development in Amazonia. Ranching dominates the region not because it successfully supplies Brazilians with beef, but rather because from the mid-1960s throughout the 1970s and most of the 1980s, the Brazilian government provided tax incentives and subsidies to corporations and small businesses that would engage in cattle ranching in Amazonia. International financial institutions, such as the World Bank and the Inter-American Bank, supported the Brazilian government's policy of promoting cattle ranching in Amazonia.

The Brazilian government promoted cattle ranching in Amazonia because it thought that it could become a leading exporter of beef on the international market. The Brazilian government and the ranchers found out that the soils on which a rain forest grows cannot provide the necessary amounts of phosphorus pasture grasses need. Within a ten-year period the phosphorus level declines to the point at which the rancher must replenish the soil with the mineral or move on. Phosphate is not an abundant mineral in Amazonia. The rancher is thus faced with the high cost of purchasing and obtaining it. In addition to the lack of adequate supplies of phosphorus in the soils, weeds and pests quickly invade pasture grasses, and cattle compact the soils, making the land susceptible to erosion.

The tax incentives and subsidies the government provided for cattle ranching in Amazonia had the effect of fueling a land rush. Once corporations and small businesses saw the economic advantages of investing in cattle ranching, others starting purchasing land in Amazonia as well. But they also saw the value in speculating in real estate and buying large tracts of lands. A government law stipulates that once a person has cleared land for pasture or farming, he or she can claim up to 50 percent more of uncleared land. This law, combined with government incentives, had the effect of triggering land speculation. Companies were not interested in cattle ranching, but in owning land in Amazonia.

The result of the government's attempts to become a major exporter of beef was a failure. Brazil remains a net importer of beef, and ranches in Amazonia do not provide enough beef to meet the demand in the region. In terms of the rain forest, experts estimate that ranching is responsible for about 72 percent of the deforestation in Amazonia. Although experts agree that pastures can be productive if managed properly, the corporations and small businesses that own the ranches are more interested in short-term economic gains over long-term investment in cattle ranching.

Mineral Extraction

Aluminum, tin, manganese, iron, gold, copper, nickel, and diamonds are the major resources of Amazonia. The largest deposit of iron ore, manganese, bauxite, copper, and nickel in the world, the Grande Carajas, is found in the state of Pará and the largest tin mine in the world, Bom Futuro, is found in the state of Rondônia. Mining and drilling, in general, can be one of the more environmentally appropriate means of economic development in Amazonia, if properly performed. Current environmental degradation and social problems associated with mining and oil drilling in Amazonia could be minimized if proper pollution regulation, planning, and management were implemented. Some of the major problems associated with these types of development are road building which increases spontaneous migration into an area; the contamination of waterways by toxic drilling muds; oil spillage; routine leaks; mercury contamination; the displacement of Amerindian groups and the transmission of diseases to them; air pollution from charcoal smelters;

and the deforestation of surrounding areas, particularly around smelters where the wood is used for fuel.

Timber/Logging

World demand for tropical timber is increasing, and along with it are timber prices. As the tropical forests in Southeast Asia are deforested, commercial logging in Amazonia will continue to grow, and the need for government controls will become more pressing. As an industry, logging is currently not a significant factor in the economy of the country. Locally, however, wood products account for 25 percent of the industrial output of four of the region's six states and federal territories.

The government of Brazil licenses the number of mills that operate in Amazonia. The number of government-licensed mills in Amazonia increased over eightfold, from 194 plants in 1965 to 1,639 plants in 1981. The increase is in part due to government tax incentives for industry to invest in Amazonian wood production. However, due to the lack of manpower and vehicles, it is easy for unlicensed mills to operate in the region.

Commercial logging in Amazonia is economically and environmentally inefficient. Lack of knowledge about the region's tropical hardwood trees is the primary obstacle to economic efficiency. Commercial loggers concentrate on traditional species of trees, such as mahogany. This species alone accounted for 84 percent of Brazil's wood exported to the United States in 1982. Foreign markets for Brazil's tropical hardwoods are narrow. In 1978, thirty-four species of trees were exported, but five species represented 90 percent of the that total.

The effect of this narrow foreign demand for traditional species has been that commercial loggers go into a part of the rain forest, harvest only those trees considered valuable on the international market, and then leave. Using the roads that the loggers have built to reach the forest, settlers move in and burn the remaining standing trees. The trees that are burned are quite valuable as wood, but they also contribute to industry in the form of nonwood products such as latexes, nuts, gums, waxes, dyes, tannins, and rattan. With the loss of the remaining mature trees, which are burned, the future of the rain forest, the immature trees growing alongside the mature ones, is also destroyed.

Hydroelectric Power

To date, three dams have, to date, been completed by the Brazilian government in Amazonia. The most recently completed, the Balbina Dam, was built in the north near the city of Manaus on the Uatumã River. It has caused the flooding of 900 square miles of forest, but produces only 250 megawatts of electricity, not enough to supply the city of Manaus (see

FIGURE 7.3

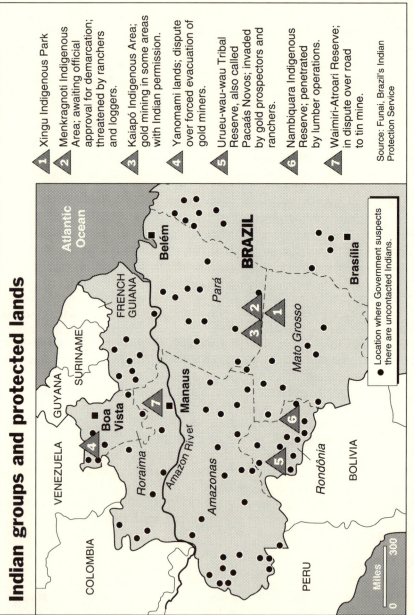

Indian groups and protected lands

1 Xingu Indigenous Park

2 Menkragnoti Indigenous Area; awaiting official approval for demarcation; threatened by ranchers and loggers.

3 Kaiapó Indigenous Area; gold mining in some areas with Indian permission.

4 Yanomami lands; dispute over forced evacuation of gold miners.

5 Urueu-wau-wau Tribal Reserve, also called Pacaás Novos; invaded by gold prospectors and ranchers.

6 Nambiquara Indigenous Reserve; penetrated by lumber operations.

7 Waimiri-Atroari Reserve; in dispute over road to tin mine.

Source: Funai, Brazil's Indian Protection Service

• Location where Government suspects there are uncontacted Indians.

Source: New York Times, 25 February 1990. Copyright © 1990 by The New York Times Company. Reprinted by permission.

Figure 7.3). Samuel Dam, on the Jamari River, was built in a low-lying area, typical of the topology of the topography of Amazonia. Because of this, engineers had to build 30 miles of dikes to help create the 2,000-square-mile lake needed for the operation of the dam. Samuel Dam produces 217 megawatts of electricity, which is insufficient to service the towns of Pôrto Velho and Ji-Paraná. The third dam, serving the Tucuruí hydroelectric plant, is on the Tocantins River. It was constructed to service the Grande Carajas Program.

The construction of the Tucuruí plant has caused the displacement of Amerindian groups from their native lands as well as environmental damage to the region. The Parakana tribe lost 5 to 10 percent of its reserve due to flooding. It was estimated that 100 to 400 other Amerindians were displaced. The flooding of the surrounding forest to create the 70-kilometer-wide reservoir was delayed by the failure of the contractors to remove rotten timber. It was discovered that some contractors cleared the forest using chemicals containing Agent Orange.

The construction of all three dams has had a destructive impact on the surrounding environment. The flooding of the forest creates stagnating waters that serve as a breeding ground for mosquitos, which infect the population with malaria. The lack of trees to hold the soils in place increases sedimentation. Sedimentation collects in the dam's reservoir, limiting the working capacity of the dam. At some point, dredging is necessary, costing more (approximately $2.50 per cubic meter) than the present value (below $2) of additional energy produced throughout a dam's life.

DISCUSSION QUESTIONS

1. *Why do you suppose most of the American development strategies are having negative effects on human standards of living? on the environment? In addressing these questions consider the different ends that drive development policies: economic growth, technological advancement, and visions of what the "good life" must be.*

2. *In this section, you have read how the World Bank and the Inter-American Bank have supported environmentally destructive development policies in Amazonia. Do you think that these international financial institutions should impose environmental requirements on the projects they fund in a country such as Brazil?*

3. *In the section on the colonization of Amazonia, you read that citizen action groups, such as international indigenous rights groups and environmental organizations, put pressure on the World Bank to stop funding Polonoroeste until environmental conditions were met by the Brazilian government. How would you feel if environmental citizen action groups from countries in*

*Europe and Latin America pressured the U.S. government into stopping the
deforestation of the ancient forests of the Pacific Northwest?*
4. *Studies of ecological trends as indicating that the human population has
breached global carrying capacity. At what level—national? international?—should policies be formulated to take into account environmental
issues?*

THE "INTERNATIONALIZATION" OF AMAZONIA

In May 1985, President Jose Sarney proposed an ambitious national land
reform plan aimed at settling 1.4 million families on 480 million hectares of
land by the year 2000. Latifundios, the expansive privately held ranches, were
to be the source of 85 percent of land. Compensation to owners would be
given in the form of government bonds redeemable in twenty years, paying a
6 percent interest rate plus inflation adjustment.

This land reform plan provoked sharp criticism and a series of battles
ensued in Congress. In October 1985, Sarney proposed a radically different
land reform bill. It called for the expropriation of government lands and no
private lands. The government lands to be expropriated were located in
Brazil's north, in the dense tropical forest. An estimated 15,000 families were
to receive land by 1986, with a total of 43 million hectares to be distributed by
1989.

Supporters of the original plan denounced the new one as a concession to
large landowners. Jose Gomes, the director of Brazil's National Institute for
Colonization and Agrarian Refore (INCRA), resigned in protest. In June
1986, Sarney signed thirty-seven decrees authorizing the first stages of land
expropriations totaling 257,125 hectares. In 1987, INCRA was ordered (by
Law 2363) to finish the allotment of plots without starting any new ones. By
1989, the land distribution program was abandoned, with only 77,351 families
having received land.

On 6 April 1989, Sarney announced his $100 million-five-year program to
zone 1.9 million square miles of Amazonia for the purposes of mining,
agriculture, and conservation, and for Amerindian reserves. The program
banned deforestation on designated protected lands. It laid out a revised tax-
incentive plan, reducing the tax credits for farming in Amazonia, and it set
regulations on the sale of mercury.[8] The plan, called "Nossa Natureza," (Our
Nature) came after several incidents placed increasing international pressure
on the Brazilian government to actively curtail development activities in
Amazonia.

The first incident was the withholding of loan funds by the Inter-American
Development Bank (IDB) in December 1987. Two loans had initially been
approved in 1986 to help finance the construction of 502 kilometers of the
road BR-364 from Pôrto Velho (Rondônia) to Rio Branco (Acre). The

project included an allocation of $10 million for social and environmental purposes. It stipulated the establishment of a reserve for rubber extraction, the demarcation of Amerindian lands, and the demarcation of conservation areas. The IDB had originally approved the loans on the ground that the people of Acre, particularly those living in the capital city, were isolated during the rainy season when the road washed out. By the end of 1987, having already disbursed $14 million of the loans, the IDB with the urging of Brazilian and foreign environmentalists, suspended payment on the loans. It was found that the Brazilian government was not complying with the environmental stipulations. It was asked to submit new plans for going forward with the environmental stipulations. A new plan was approved by the end of June 1989. The resumption of funds were conditional upon six-month reviews to verify that the Brazilian government was complying with the environmental conditions.

In December 1988, a Brazilian rubber tapper, Chico Mendes, was killed near his home in the state of Acre. Mendes had become involved in organizing rubber tappers to take measures to preserve the rain forest as rubber preserves. The state of Acre was beginning to experience the effects of the deforestation that accompanies cattle ranching. In an effort to protect unclaimed parts of the forest, rubber tappers organized peaceful sit-ins, thwarting attempts by ranchers to invade unmarked forest areas. The activities of Mendes and the rubber tappers brought them international attention—which eventually encompassed the construction of the last leg of BR-364, that is, Rio Branco (Acre) to the highway system of Peru. (Due to lack of funds and the difficulty of constructing a highway in the Andes, Peru has yet to construct a highway linking its Pacific coastal cities with the interior.) Mendes actively campaigned to stop the IDB from paving BR-364 between Pôrto Velho and Rio Branco. He traveled to Washington, D.C., and lobbied against further road construction. Funding was temporarily suspended.

After Mendes's death, international attention focused on the Brazilian government's efforts to secure external financing for the last leg of BR-364 (Acre-Pacific). Japanese investors expressed interest in financing the highway because it would give them Pacific coast access to Acre's tropical hardwoods. The U.S. government publicly asked the Japanese not to invest in the construction of the highway because it would open up the region to spontaneous migration and deforestation. After some consideration, the World Bank has gone ahead and has approved loans for the construction of the final leg of BR-364.

On 10 March 1989, an international conference on the environment was convened at the Hague. Although Brazil had been invited to attend, Sarney personally boycotted the conference on the ground that Amazonia was a domestic issue, not an international one. Sarney stated, "We are masters of our destiny and will not permit any interference in our territory."[9]

Due to the environmental destruction associated with its three existing hydroelectric dams, the World Bank withheld the granting of $500 million loan to Eletrobras for future construction of dams. The World Bank was primarily concerned that Brazil would use the funds to expand its nuclear power capabilities without proper guidelines. In June 1989, the Brazilian government declared that it would no longer seek to obtain the loan.

Events such as those described above led to the development of Sarney's "Nossa Natureza" program. Its aim was to permit the "rational siting of economic activities" and "the environmental monitoring of these activities" in the Amazon region. The program includes forty-nine environmental decrees. These decrees cover a variety of projects, such as the demarcation and management of national biological and nature reserves. Brazilians and foreigners alike have criticized the program on several grounds. First, it fails to end the credits for agriculture, particularly farm projects. (The tax incentives for cattle ranching were recently terminated by the Brazilian government.) Second, it fails to provide pollution guidelines for charcoal-fueled smelters in Amazonia. Third, the surveying and demarcating of reserves and nature preserves requires funding and the necessary manpower that Brazil lacks at this point in time. Fourth, even though some Amerindian lands have been demarcated, in many instances the government has neither officially decreed formal possession of the land to the Indians nor has it taken any enforcement measures to keep invaders off the land.

It is widely recognized that Brazil's economic difficulties are a major obstacle to the success of its environmental program. Well aware of the shortage of funds, Sarney asked other countries and nonprofit organizations to contribute to a fund specifically established to support the plan. He asked countries to stop criticizing Brazil for its unwillingness to engage in debt-for-nature loans and to do something to help Brazil enforce its environmental program. To underscore the critical lack of funds, the employees of the newly established Brazilian Institute for the Environment and Renewable Natural Resources (IBAMA), which is responsible for "formulating, coordinating, executing and enforcing the national environmental policy, as well as for managing renewable natural resources," walked off the job in June 1989 to protest the lack of funds and clear direction from the Brazilian government.

At the same time as the Nossa Natureza program was officially announced, the World Bank announced that it would loan $300 million to Brazil for projects in parts of the country other than Amazonia to ease the pressure on the Brazilian government to continue development in Amazonia. In the summer of 1990, the World Bank granted IBAMA an $8 million low-interest loan (matched by an appropriation by the Brazilian government) to be be used in its fire-prevention program. In addition, the current government of President Collor de Mello is negotiating with the Inter-American Bank for a $5.3 million loan to help the Brazilian government establish a series of reserves in Amazonia.

The current administration is facing a worsening economic situation. This in turn creates internal pressures to continue to develop Amazonia as it was developed in the past, through capital-intensive, export-oriented strategies. But traditional means of development, such as farming and ranching, are showing diminishing economic returns. Alternatives need to be found. It is clear that with its large foreign debt, inflationary economy, and an increasing poor majority, Brazil needs financial assistance, scientific expertise, and development recommendations to engage in environmentally sound development in Amazonia.

DISCUSSION QUESTIONS

1. *What forms of foreign intervention are morally justified to pressure or coerce Brazil into protecting the natural resources of Amazonia and the indigenous peoples who live there? What forms are not morally justified? Why? Are the "action plans" attached to loans by the World Bank and the Inter-American Development Bank legitimate forms of intervention?*
2. *How do we determine whether or not public lands in a country such as Brazil are international common goods? Is it the scarcity of the resource? The benefits of that resource for humankind?*
3. *How does the status of the Brazilian rain forest as a public good compare with other so-called common goods, such as the Antarctic, the atmosphere, or the ocean floors?*
4. *Would the cosmopolitan argue that the rain forest has to first be designated a common good before distributive justice claims on the part of outsiders can be made?*
5. *Should there be an international environmental regime responsible for monitoring, regulating, and enforcing deforestation laws? Or should more funding, expertise, and attention be given to local and regional citizens's participation groups within Brazil? within the nine countries that share the Amazonian rain forests?*

NOTES

1. Fundacao Instituto Brasileiro de Geografia e Estastica (IBGE), *Anuario Estatistico do Brasil 1989*, Brazil, 1989.
2. The figures vary slightly according to the source. John O. Browder, "Public Policy and Deforestation in the Brazilian Amazon," in *Public Policy and the Misuse of Forest Resources*, Robert Repetto and Malcolm Gillis, eds. (Cambridge, Mass.: Cambridge University Press, 1988), p. 247; Dennis Mahar,

Government Policies and Deforestation in Brazil's Amazon Region (Washington, D.C.: World Bank, 1989), p. 3.

3. The Brady Plan, announced in March 1989, asks U.S. commercial banks to voluntarily reduce the debt of Third World countries. In conjunction with this voluntary debt reduction, the IMF and the World Bank are being asked to support the plan by implementing changes in their lending policies. In order to qualify for debt reduction, a country has to engage in sound fiscal policies that will attract back foreign investors into the country, encourage domestic savings, and promote the return of flight capital.

4. Former president Jose Sarney quoted in "Brazil Angrily Unveils Plan for Amazon," by Eugene Robinson, *Washington Post* 7 April 1989.

5. Richard House, "Brazil Declines Invitation to Conference on Ecology: Sarney Fears Amazon will be Singled Out." *The Washington Post* 4 March 1989.

6. World Resources Institute, *World Resources Report 1990-91*. In collaboration with the United Nations Environment Programme and the United Nations Development Programme (Oxford: Oxford University Press, 1990), pp. 102-103.

7. Dennis Mahar, *Government Policies and Deforestation in Brazil's Amazon Region* (Washington, D.C.: World Bank, 1989), p. 7.

8. James Bruinsma, "Environmental Law: Brazil Enacts New Protections for the Amazon Rain Forest," *Harvard International Law Journal* 30, no. 1 (1989): 503-513.

9. Richard House, "Brazil Declines Invitation."

FURTHER READING ON BRAZIL

Books

Anderson, Anthony. *Alternatives to Deforestation*. New York: Columbia University Press, 1990.

Browder, John O., "Public Policy and Deforestation in the Brazilian Amazon," *Public Policies and the Misuse of Forest Resources*, Robert Repetto and Malcolm Gillis. Cambridge: Cambridge University Press, 1988.

Hecht, Susanna B. "Cattle Ranching in Amazonia: Political and Ecological Considerations," in *Frontier Expansion in Amazonia*. Marianna Schminck and Charles Wood, eds. Gainesville, Fla.: University of Florida Press, 1984.

_____. *The Fate of the Forest: Developers, Destroyers and Defenders of the Amazon*. With Alexander Cockburn, London: Verso, 1989.

Mahar, Dennis J. "Development of the Brazilian Amazon: Prospects for the 1980s," in *The Dilemma of Amazonian Development*, ed. by Emilio Moran (Boulder, Colo.: Westview Press, 1983).

_____. *Frontier Development Policy in Brazil: A Study of Amazonia.* New York: Praeger, 1979.

_____. *Government Policies and Deforestation in Brazil's Amazon Region.* Washington, D.C.: World Bank, 1989.

Myers, Norman. *Conversion of Moist Tropical Forests.* Washington, D.C.: The National Academy of Science, 1980.

_____. *Natural Resource Systems and Human Exploitation Systems: Physiobiotic and Ecological Linkages,* Environmental Department Working Paper no. 12. Washington, D.C.: World Bank, November 1988.

World Bank. *The World Bank and the Environment. First Annual Report 1990,* Washington, D.C.: World Bank, 1990.

World Resources Institute. *World Resources Report 1990-91.* In collaboration with the United Nations Environment Programme and the United Nations Development Programme. Oxford: Oxford University Press, 1990.

Articles

Brooke, James, "Harvesting Exotic Crops to Save Brazil's Forest." *New York Times,* April 30, 1990.

Bruinsma, James, "Environmental Law: Brazil Enacts New Protections for the Amazon Rain Forest," *Harvard International Law Journal* 30, no. 1 (1989): 503-513.

Fearnside, Philip, "Deforestation in Brazilian Amazônia: The Rates and Causes," *The Ecologist* 19, no. 6. (1989): 214-218.

Guppy, Nicholas, "Tropical Deforestation: A Global View." *Foreign Affairs* 62, no. 4 (1984): 928-965.

Hecht, Susanna B. "The Sacred Cow in the Green Hell." *The Ecologist* 19, no. 6. (1989): 229-234.

Maxwell, Kenneth, "The Tragedy of the Amazon," *New York Review of Books* vol. 38, no. 5 (1991): 24-29.

Repetto, Robert, "Deforestation in the Tropics." *Scientific American* (April 1990): 36-42.

Treece, David, "The Militarization and Industrialization of Amazônia: The Calha Norte and Grande Carajas Programmes." *The Ecologist* 19, no. 6 (1989): 225-228.

ABOUT THE BOOK
AND EDITOR

In just the past few years, both the theoretical importance and the practical necessity of ethical analyses in international affairs have become well established. In order to more closely examine particular ethical dilemmas, Rachel McCleary has put together a collection of carefully selected case studies illustrating the variety of ethical concerns that arise in international affairs.

As in every volume in the Case Studies in International Affairs series, this volume opens with an introduction that gives students the philosophical background and theoretical framework they need to understand the cases that follow. Individual introductions to each case place the study in context relative to the other studies and to the overall theme of the volume. Discussion questions round out the treatment of the issues, prompting explorations beyond the cases themselves.

The cases in *Seeking Justice* range from questions about the U.S. invasion of Panama to the withdrawal from Vietnam, from the uneven application of the Law of the Sea to the equally uneven distribution of trade favors emerging from the integration of the European Community. Considerations of economic justice are also the focus of a case on the IMF and Nigeria.

A Brazilian case study brings together several issues implicit in the earlier cases—the nature of state sovereignty, the status of moral obligations and rights in the international arena, and the structural inequality of international regimes. This study shows how the issues of debt, development, and environment are integrally linked and pinpoints the kinds of ethical problems policymakers, experts, and theorists will be wrestling with in the near future.

The cases have been selected and presented to help students identify the issues and make connections between disparate sets of circumstances without spoonfeeding interpretation or analysis. Rachel McCleary skillfully presents the spectrum of ethical questions posed by international events and reveals the dialectical interplay among them.

Rachel M. McCleary is program officer for the Grants and Education and Training Programs at the United States Institute of Peace. She has published numerous articles on ethics and foreign affairs with a special emphasis on Latin America.